Hercules

Hercules the Guardian of the Hot Gates

(The Legendary Stories of Ancient Greece's Most Famous Heroes)

Fatima Runte

Published By **Ryan Princeton**

Fatima Runte

All Rights Reserved

Hercules: Hercules the Guardian of the Hot Gates (The Legendary Stories of Ancient Greece's Most Famous Heroes)

ISBN 978-1-77485-933-9

No part of this guidebook shall be reproduced in any form without permission in writing from the publisher except in the case of brief quotations embodied in critical articles or reviews.

Legal & Disclaimer

The information contained in this ebook is not designed to replace or take the place of any form of medicine or professional medical advice. The information in this ebook has been provided for educational & entertainment purposes only.

The information contained in this book has been compiled from sources deemed reliable, and it is accurate to the best of the Author's knowledge; however, the Author cannot guarantee its accuracy and validity and cannot be held liable for any errors or omissions. Changes are periodically made to this book. You must consult your doctor or get professional medical advice before using any of the suggested remedies, techniques, or information in this book.

Upon using the information contained in this book, you agree to hold harmless the Author from and against any damages, costs, and expenses, including any legal fees potentially resulting from the application of any of the information provided by this guide. This disclaimer applies to any damages or injury caused by the use and application, whether directly or indirectly, of any advice or information presented, whether for breach of contract, tort, negligence, personal injury, criminal intent, or under any other cause of action.

You agree to accept all risks of using the information presented inside this book. You need to consult a professional medical practitioner in order to ensure you are both able and healthy enough to participate in this program.

Table of contents

Chapter 1: A Noble Lineage And A Difficult Birth 1

Chapter 2: Growing Pains 32

Chapter 3: Triumph And Madness 60

Chapter 4: Hercules At Work 90

Chapter 5: Hero At Work 125

Chapter 1: A Noble Lineage And A Difficult Birth

Our story begins when a maiden is tied to a boulder. This is not any maiden. The nature of these stories requires that the victim be a princess. The legend is silent about the subject. However, later artists Rembrandt and Titian will have fevered fantasies that demand the naked princess.

This is not any princess. But the famous Andromeda, princesse of Aethiopia. Andromeda's beauty, her untold beauty, has made her a failure. Andromeda's mother was proud and extolled her daughter's beauty. The mother could have stopped there and Andromeda and the beauty she exhibited would have been forgotten by all generations. But her mother did not only praise her daughter for her beauty, but for her ability to see the seas.

The proud mother also boasted to Ocean that her daughter looked better than the Neriads. These were the sea-nymphs and daughters of Poseidon. While such beauty contests by proxy are not uncommon among parents of nubile girls, it can be dangerous when one of their parents is the Lords the Sea, a senior god with an angry and proud disposition. Poseidon was insulted by the idea that his offspring might have been considered inferior to mere mortals.

The strange creature Poseidon found in his watery domain included a monster called Cetus. Cetus is actually a monstrous because large sea creatures used to be called Cetus. This is why modern whales are called Cetaceans. Cetus was a kind of rampaging amphibian and lived on the same land as the sea. Cetus began to destroy Aethiopia's coastline, following Poseidon's directives.

The modern Ethiopia of today is landlocked and this makes it difficult to do. However, the Aethiopia in myth was more expansive. The coastline of the kingdom extended to the Mediterranean up to Joppa. Joppa was the modern Jaffa. It is not only famous for oranges but also has strong cetacean connections. Joppa is the place where Cetus was seen, and it's also the place where Jonah, a prophet from a different culture, traveled to find his fate in a whale.

Cetus had an ulterior motive for his trip. The deal was made by the kings and queens of Aethiopia with Poseidon to save their country. The agreement stipulated that the monster would stop his ravages by performing one more act of violence. Andromeda was to be killed and devoured. As Andromeda spoke to her parents, one can see a level of terseness as they struggled with their emotions while standing beside the rock. Andromeda, however, was not able to wait for her fate.

Perseus is the son of Danae and the heir to Argos's throne. Perseus did not want another adventure at that time, since he had just killed Medusa (the blood of the Medusa became the venomous serpents of Africa). But no hero could ignore Cetus's monstrous figure rising slowly from the depths or the shriek that Andromeda made at her imminent doom.

Perseus may have been able to pass on unseen as he was as invisible under his feet as the air underneath him. Perseus wore the winged sandals he borrowed from Hermes in his mission to slay Medusa. The helm of Hades made him (and Death) virtually invisible. Perseus was only one of the winged beings that soared above Joppa. Eros could also see him.

Perseus fell for the chained maiden, but he was unerringly nailed with one shot from Eros' bow. The only options for Perseus were to either endure a brief, tragic love affair or do something drastic about Cetus who was quickly approaching.

For look! The breast of the monster rolls the waves away like a galley that furrows the sea with its pointed prow as rowers sweat and strain.

Ovid, the Roman poet, takes the tale as it is. Cetus was closing in upon his helpless prey. Perseus, like any good Greek boy, quickly presented his case before his parents. Perseus spoke in a few words to his parents, saying, "It is me or the Monster, and frankly, she could not do more. If she takes me she could make worse." Cetus was literally a stone's-throw away.

He was no farther from the rock now than Balearic missile slingers can throw their flying missiles across to the sky. But Perseus leapt from the ground to fly into the sky. The monster saw his shadow in the sea and began to savage what it saw.

Perseus dived down through the air toward the creature's shoulder and sank its crescent blade into its shoulder. The beast roared from its wounds and stood straight up, high above the air. It then dived below water, and then it turned in frenzy as a fierce boar when there was a hunting pack nearby.

Perseus, with his quick wings, manages to evade the snapping jaws. He then plunges the sharpened sword between his ribs, into his monstrous back. The back is all rough and barnacles. The creature vomits sea spray and purple-colored blood together and the sandals worn by Perseus' feet are so soaked that they can no longer be trusted. He sees the rock lying in the water, but it is still awash in the turbulence. He stands with his left arm braced against a ridge as he steadyes himself and begins to stab at the monster's groin.

Ovid Metamorphoses 4.80ff

According to some accounts, Andromeda was freed by Eros herself. Perseus made himself look presentable by cleaning his blood-drenched body from a nearby stream. (Later Roman tourists paid good prices to see that stream. It was still reddened due to an algal bloom. They also saw the Rock of Andromeda as well as the grooves created by the chains.

Andromeda is Pursues. Cetus with Andromeda.

Detail from an 18th-century oil painting by Charles-Antoine Coypel.

Joppa is standing on a hill with a rock in front. These men point out the marks that chains made when Andromeda was held on to the rock.

Pliny The Elder, Natural History 5. 69

It was not all bad, however. The former fiancee of Andromeda violently opposed the sudden alteration of wedding plans. Perseus, however, made the man furious by showing Medusa's head. The power of Medusa had not been revoked. This incident aside, Perseus and Andromeda found true love.

Perseus, though he was indeed a prince and returned home to claim his birthright of becoming king at Argos, never did. Instead, while on a trip through central Greece, he lost his cap and found mushrooms growing in the area where it had fallen. Perseus founded a new city from this spot, "Mycenae" in Greek. Perseus's children would become leaders and legends in the region. The city was the best in Greece during later years.

Perseus is still with Andromeda, and they are now together as constellations of the northern sky. Perseus is still holding the head of Medusa. Now, Perseus's eye is the star Agol. Maybe he does it to avoid the in-laws. Andromeda's parents Cepheus & Cassiopeia have moved into adjacent constellations. Poseidon did exact his final vengeance on Cassiopeia, for Cassiopeia is staring into the night with her head towards The Pole Star. So as the stars move through space, the boastful queen is destined to spend half her night upside-down.

Dynastic relations

Millennia earlier than the Montagues & Capulets, the Pelopids & the Perseids existed. Today, the Perseids meteorite-shower that lights up the August night sky is what is most famous about the Perseids. Named after the constellation Perseus, the meteorites appear from the direction of Perseus.

Perseids, who were Perseus's children in the heroic age, were a powerful force on the peninsula. The accursed Pelopids repelled this dominant position. Accursed is not an informal pejorative, but a literal fact. Tantalus was the patriarch and founder of the Pelopid family. He once gave the Gods a memorable meal, but we won't get into his details. This meal was primarily his son Pelops. The portions were cut and served with beans, and a nice ambrosia. Demeter, the corn goddess and god of the corn, however, took a bite. Demeter was upset as Persephone was just abducted by Hades, and had raped her daughter Persephone. Tantalus was exiled from Tartarus for this and other misdeeds. This was a maximum security prison for cosmic undesirables. Tantalus suffered the torture of having food and drink always within his reach. It is not from the meal Tantalus served the Gods that the word 'tantalize' comes, but from this punishment.

Pelops was revived, with an ivory shoulder replacing Demeter's main dish. Pelops' name, which means "the dark one", was later used to describe his relationship with Hippodamia. Hippodamia is a relative of Perseus. Pelops also had the task of convincing his father-inlaw to marry him. This father-inlaw was King Oneomaus who was himself a hateful character. He was known for challenging his daughter's suitors as chariot racers and executioning them when they lost. Pelops replaced the parts that held together Oneomaus' chariot with beeswax-based substitutes to make sure he didn't suffer this fate. Oneomaus, however, died in the subsequent race day crash. His charioteer, however survived. Pelops then threw the charioteer off a rock to silence him. There were two outcomes to this deed. Two things were positive. On one side, Pelops won a race, got married, and took the vacant throne. The race's success was remembered in a sporting festival that was later expanded (by Hercules), to become the Olympic Games.

Pelops was a great ruler. The land he ruled over has since been called the "Peloponnese." Perseus, the only obstacle to Pelops' total dominance of the peninsula, was something that Pelops couldn't overcome. Pelops' efforts to dominate the peninsula were also hampered due to the negative consequences from his victory. Pelops had cursed the killer of the charioteer he had thrown off a cliff.

The curse did not apply to Pelops alone, but to the entire clan. Pelop's second wife Hippodamia committed suicide, and the family line was marked by incestuous cannibalism and fratricide. Agamemnon, the husband of Pelop, died after he had killed his child.

Because of Nicippe, the Star-crossed Pelopids can be relevant to the story about Hercules. Nicippe was born to Hippodamia just before her mother died. She later married Perseid, a Perseid (a son of Andromeda's and Perseus' called Sthenelus). This marriage was among a variety of dynastic matches. It occurred when Perseids, Pelopids, made love not war and transferred their rivalry onto the marriage bed.

As might be expected from a Perseid ruler and prince, Sthenelus led a busy, complex life. He was able to drive into exile Amphitryon (a man who had killed Sthenelus' brother) and he was engaged in marriage to his niece, Alcmene. Sthenelus had no idea of it but this act set off a chain reaction that was to move rivalry for Mycenaean royalties from the Peloponnese and into the heavens. It also took the Pelops and Perseus families to the Olympian gods.

The births of Hercules, and Eurystheus

Alcmene was an exceptional woman in beauty and form. In intellect, no mortal woman could match her. Her face and dark eyes were equally persuasive as Aphrodite's.

Hesiod 1,1 The Shield of Heracles

So the poet describes Amphitryon's granddaughter Perseus and Sthenelus, who is also the betrothed to him. This is why Amphitryon was a formidable spear-wielding warlord. The Taphosites were the first to be persuaded by the love-struck swain. Alcmene had a justified grudge against these people, since they had killed her brother. The Taphains resided in northwestern Greece. It was a long and complex war that deserved an epic. (Although it was epic, there isn't enough space here to recount the story of battles and lust that kept Amphitryon in the arms his beloved. Amphitryon escaped with victory from his war and raced home to celebrate it with Alcmene.

Zeus was the chief danger to Zeus' beautiful princess status in Heroic Greco. Danae, the great-grandmother Alcmene's mother and mother of Perseus had realized that Zeus was not protected by being in a tower. Zeus, who was married to Hera, his sister, had few reservations about incest and shared his love for her with his children. In fact, he is one the few creatures outside the genus curniculis (rabbit clan) that has managed to be his great-uncle.

According to Hesiod's poem, Alcmene was so attached to her Amphitryon that he would not allow her to look at any other man. Zeus knew all this and so began his seduction with Alcmene, by changing himself into Amphitryon. As Alcmene's beloved, he disguised himself to appear as Amphitryon and returned from the wars in a hurry. He also carried a Taphian cup as evidence of his success.

What has happened in the army?... Zeus now talks to Alcmene. She thinks that she is actually with her lover. Zeus is now telling how he routed his enemy host and how he took a fortune from booty. Amphitryon took the loot and it has been stolen from him. Zeus will get whatever he desires.

Plautus, the Roman playwright, depicts Hermes in the prologue of Amphitryon.

The night that followed was indeed mythical. There were multiple bouts intense sex and long anecdotes in between, where Zeus/Amphitryon shared the stories of his alter ego from the wars. Alcmene said that the night spent in lovemaking and story-telling seemed longer than three normal nights. Zeus was enjoying far too good an experience to pack it in the morning, so he used the King of Gods' prerogative to extend the night until Alcmene and presumably Alcmene were satisfied.

Unexpected side-effect to this night of unnaturally long epic sex was the unexpected. Alcmene was able to get pregnant. The same egg was also fertilized multiple times by the Zeus seed. The new child received more divine strength and divine essence with each iteration. Zeus was able to see that the result would surpass his other remarkable offspring.

Alcmene didn't stop the reproductive process. Amphitryon returned home from wars the very next day, and immediately put his beloved to bed. The truth emerged when Alcmene commented, perhaps on Alcmene's partner's unique technique or endurance.

It was too late. Alcmene, the son Zeus, shared Alcmene's womb now with Amphitryon's son. This process is known as heteroparental Superfecundation. Even though all seemed well, Zeus was so excited at the potential of this son he had just given birth that he refused to speak. Zeus announced the birth of Perseus when it was due. He would now be the ruler of Mycenae & the Peloponnese.

Enter Hera. She is the future curse of Hercules' existence and Queen of the Gods. Hera was aware and bitterly hurt by her husband's many infidelities. Zeus was King of the Gods. He was Hera's husband. Zeus was unpunished so, according to one Roman writer, 'if the donkey isn't beating you, you get on the saddle'. Hera, furious at her husband's affairs, took aim at his partners, however unwilling they may have been, and punished all their children, regardless of how innocent.

This was an experience that every Roman and ancient Greek would have known. Seneca, a Roman writer, wrote that "to take the mistress of a husband is a grave offence against a wife." (Letters 95.37) Everyone knew about the injustice of punishing a slave for her rape by her master but not everyone understood it. The tragedy of Hera's victims was real to the Romans (Greek Letters 95.37).

Princesses suffered in the exact same way as slaves.

Alcmene was pregnant by Alcmene. Her unborn child was the victim of the powerful deity's deadly vindictiveness. Innocence didn't excuse them from the punishment. Hercules was the victim of circumstances, as was his mother. The Greeks, Romans and others who followed Hercules' story mainly did so to understand how he coped.

(Graeco Romans believed that no man could be responsible for the life that was dealt to him. However, the way he played that hand gave an indication of the man. Hera was certain that Zeus' savage son would never become the king of Mycenae, and the Peloponnese. Zeus had already said that Perseus' heir would be king that day. This would happen because Zeus is a Greek god.

Integrity in modern times is a virtue. He says what he thinks, does what he does. There can be no misinterpretation of his thoughts, words or actions. They are both integral, which explains the term 'integrity'. Integrity may be admirable in a human being. But integrity when you are an allpowerful god is a curse. You only need to think about a thing. Your divine power will make it happen. Being a God means that you are not able to change your actions and therefore cannot say sorry. It is obvious that the universe would soon become chaotic if Gods were to second-guess themselves. Integrity and inability go back to correct errors are key factors in the mythical Olympian Gods' notoriously bad impulse control.

Integrity in the case Hercules meant that Zeus declared that Perseus's son would be king and that the matter was final. It would happen, regardless of the circumstances. Hera now had just two options. One was Eileithyia, the goddess who was, according to some, Hera's little girl. The second card was that Zeus did not specify which Perseus-related descendant would be the king. The Pelopid Nicippe (p.6) was a daughter of Perseus.

This is how the goddess Eileithyia entered the picture, as Eileithyia (the Goddess of Childbirth) was born. Eileithyia had the final say on whether a baby was quick and easy or long and painful. Homer described her as 'Hera's child, who holds power over bitter pangs during childbirth'. (Homer Iliad 11.270).

After Hera had given her directions, Eileithyia made it a matter of minutes to suspend the birth of Alcmene's baby. It left Alcmene exhausted and unable to bear the pains of another unsuccessful labour. Alcmene suffered but Eileithyia went to Mycenae and incited Nicippe to have a speedy, productive birth despite the fact that her child was two months premature. Eurystheus, a son of Nicippe & Sthenelus, was born. He was also the grandson Of Perseus & Andromeda as well as the king of Mycenae via birth and Zeus' word. The son of Zeus was the other grandson and he remained in the Alcmene-tortured womb for as long as Hera, Eileithyia, were concerned.

Alcmene sweated it on for seven whole days. If it weren't for her nurse, Alcmene might have suffered even longer. Galinthias a childhood friend of Alcmene, and herself of semidivine origin was the nurse. Galinthias, who was of supernatural origin, noticed Eileithyia's presence at the bedside. This made it clear that the goddess was not there to help but hinder.

Galinthias could also contact mystic beings who no mortal could access. This was another advantage of being semidivine.

Galinthias, who was at the bedside her friend, ran through secret passageways to reach the cave that the Fates had created. There were threads that described the fate of every living creature. Galinthias was able to find Clotho, a spinner, who held on to the thread to weave Alcmene's unborn baby into the web. Loudly, the nurse declared that Alcmene's child was born through the will of Zeus. Clotho was so stunned by the announcement, that she released her grip on thread. This thread quickly grew into the web and was irrevocably a part the tapestry. Eileithyia's death had been avoided, and the child was now born, though it was too late to claim his inheritance.

Galinthias was deceitful and brought two children into this world. When Amphitryon returned home from the wars, he had slept the night with Alcmene. This was the same day that Zeus had slept with

Alcmene. Both sessions had proved fruitful. Amphitryon was proud to be the father of his son, Iphicles. However, he also became the reluctant stepfather for Zeus' offspring.

(Incidentally Amphitryon was so traumatized at the whole matter that he never slept in his bed again with Alcmene. Alcmene's sexual relationship with Amphitryon was not ended there. Zeus was unable to have sex with any other mortal woman after that, and he claimed - somewhat ambiguously – that he had outdone Alcmene.

Hera had achieved her purpose, for Eurystheus (son of Nicippe), was the descendant to Perseus. Eurystheus became the future king and queen of Mycenae by taking over from Zeus. Hera was not satisfied with the result of her husband's affair. Galinthias, Galinthias' nurse, was punished brutally for allowing the child be born. Galinthias became a polecat, a creature once feared for its incontinence.

Actually, this revenge was a bit of a fail because Hecate, the witch goddess, had a soft place for the underdog (or undergod) and adopted the weasel/nurse to her retinue. This resulted in Hecate adopting the pet weasel into her household.

For the child, the Queen decided to take the brat out of the world again after he had entered the world despite Hera's best efforts. Galinthias is replaced as nurse by Amphitryon.

I'll now let you in on something even more extraordinary. Two huge crested serpents, which were enormously large, swam through the skylight as the boy lay in the cradle. Instantly, both of them raised their heads and began looking around. They quickly headed towards the cradle once they had located the children. I was terrified for the children, and scared for myself. I backtracked, pulling the cradle up and rocking it around, but the snakes continued to pursue me. The children saw the snakes and ran towards them.

Plautus Amphitryon 5.1

The fact that a newborn baby could use large serpents for cradle toys and end up crushing them in the process meant that his ancestry couldn't be hidden. Even though it was futile, it was still necessary to appease Hera. Gods and men both gave it a try.

Alcmene had given his infant name to Alcides, a combination word from Alaceus who was the father of Tiryns (the town where he was born), and Alaceus. (That town still exists today, its walls are intact, though they have been significantly damaged by the passage of thirty one centuries. Alcmene changed this name to Heracles'. This, which is the Greek form for 'Hercules", means glory of Lady'. ('Hera' means Lady' and is the feminine version of the word 'Hero'. The goddess did not feel very glorified when the child she had as a result of her husbands extra-marital affairs was a bastard. Hera felt even more angry when her name was used to draw attention to her humiliation.

Alcmene's immature attempt at flattery was a failure. The attempt of the Gods to do the same did not go well. Athena is believed to have devised the plan. This is a clear indication that even the Goddess Wisdom has her off days. Hermes would bring the baby to Hera, then place the child at her side. Hera would eventually wake up and discover she was feeding a suckling baby. Hopefully, this would increase her maternal instincts and make her more compassionate toward the child. Even if Hera failed to awaken her maternal instincts, the child could still get some Hera milk. The combination of the child's divine heritage and Hercules would make Hercules even more demigod.

Hera was astonished to find a tiny baby at her breast when Hera awoke. Hera allowed the child to continue eating because she was sympathetic to his apparent hunger. Hera then realized that the baby had extracted her milk with such force and vigour that Hera could not tell who it was. Hera then ripped the child from her arms so violently that her milk flew away to the heavens. This milk can still be found in the heavens today. Romans called it Via Lactea, or the 'Milky Way'. This is Greek for "the circle of Milk", galaxias, kyklos which means the galaxy.

Hera, unwitting wet nurse

Johan Niclas Bystromin, sculpture at Royal Palace, Stockholm

Chapter 2: Growing Pains

Alcmene was not surprising to be upset about having fallen prey to a powerful goddess. Amphitryon, who was still in the city at the time, had again upset the hosts. The couple, now exiled once again, made their way to Thebes in central Greece.

To the left is the Elektran Gate, you will see the remains of an ancient house. According to them, Amphitryon is believed to have lived here while exiled to Tiryns.... The rooms of Alcmene remain plainly visible among the ruins.

Pausanias Guide to Greece 9. 11. 1

Alcmene was finally settled in her new home and decided that her only option was to let go of the child who had so utterly destroyed her life. She chose exposure, which one historian brutally calls 'postnatal birth control'. The ancient world had no reliable birth control method so unwanted children were all around. It was common to leave these unwanted children at the gates of the city, in a market or on a field. The child could then be adopted by anyone interested as if it were a kitten. The baby would starve if not picked up on time.

Athena is the first to point out this potentially disastrous development. It is unclear how Zeus would respond. Athena may have felt a little guilty for not being able to bring Hera around. Hercules is still something Hera hates. However, Hera was able to absorb some of her milk. He became officially a demigod. Either this or

Athena's fondness for rogues and thuggish people, Athena would eventually become a mentor to Hercules, both now and later.

She brought the baby back to Alcmene's field and gave him a message to her, perhaps warning him not to make the same mistake again. Pausanias, a writer about a thousand year later, published the first ever travel guide for ancient Roman tourists visiting Greece. He points the traveller outside of Thebes to the field 'The field Of Heracles', where the incident took place. (Pausanias 9.25.2). A poet is now reciting the tale of Hercules' boyhood.

Amphitryon's son, Amphitryon from Argos, grew in front of his mother like a seedling plant planted in a vineyard. He learned his letters through a sleepless mentor and a hero, the older Linus, son of Apollo.

Eurytus taught him to bend a bow and fire arrows at mark. This was a man born rich and with great domains... all the tricks of Argos' wrestlers and of boxers who are skilled with the hand-strap.

Theocritus Ityll 24.103

It is interesting that Alcmene selected the tutors for the best era. Later ages would view Hercules only as a solitary hero, who did solo missions. The ancient Greeks understood Hercules to have been a strong commander and general, who was capable of leading armies and conquering cities. Castor, a demigod who is part of the constellation Gemini's 'Castor' ('The Twins") taught Hercules these skills. Castor taught Hercules the following: "How to marshal company, measure an invading squadron and give orders for his own troop on horse."

Hercules got the education that a young aristocratic boy would receive. It was not the education of an old aristocrat because the universe of his day was too chaotic and ready for formal educational curricula. Hercules received the education of the younger aristocrats, who heard his stories in the theatre and to the rhythm of a guitar. Aristocratic Graeco Roman boys must learn the arts, as well poetry and war. They also needed to master the art of estate management. Perhaps this was something Hercules learned from Amphitryon. Amphitryon was a Greek aristocrat who taught Hercules how race a chariot. We also learn about the close relationship between Hercules, Amphitryon, and how Hercules moved his bed so that he could share a room in his bedroom with his stepfather. Hercules was then accepted as one among the leaders among the young men from his adoptive town.

The Hercules home of the Hercules family

Detail from a Roman painting dating back to the 1st century AD, found at Pompeii

The following is the custom, according to what I know. This article was published in AD 150. A boy must be handsome, strong, and have noble birth to become a priest of Isthmian Apollo. He is also known as the Laurelbearer. The boys wear laurel wreaths, which Apollo considered sacred. I am not certain that all laurel bearers are faithful to the tradition of dedicating a bronze tripod to God. In fact, I doubt it. However, the more wealthy boys will dedicate them. Amphitryon gifted a tripod on behalf of Heracles, not only because it is old but also because of its fame as a dedication.

Pausanias Guides to Greece 9.10.4

We find it remarkable that all of Hercules' teachers were powerful and respected in their time. Now that they are old, the teachers act as tutors to young Hero. He inherits their talents and combines all the skills to become the sum of all his talents. Regrettably, not every skill was acquired in the exact same way. His most powerful advocates never described Hercules, but he was a scholar and gentleman.

Hercules only ever achieved proficiency with the bow as a stringed musical instrument. Linus, Linus's music teacher at the time, was very frustrated by Hercules' inability to master the bow. Linus was well-known as the creator of melody. He had the misfortune to spend his genius on someone who couldn't even carry a tune in one bucket. Linus gave the difficult final session to his student a huge wallop using his lyre. This struck a chord with the youth, who returned to it full of interest. A typical teacher-student con-temps. However, Hercules did show the same mighty strength he had even then. Linus was crushed to a grape.

Linus was not forgotten, even though he is gone. He is the name behind a number of remarkable characters, such as the second pope (the successor to St Peter), to a Charlie Brown comic book character. Linus Torvals's namesake is also him. Linux, the operating system that bears his name, has it.

Hercules was accused of homicide because he had removed such a notable personage from the planet. Linus was not the first of the many corpses Hercules would leave scattered throughout the mythical landscape. It is possible that Linus also killed one of his tutors. However, this was not considered an accident. Linus' trial was overturned by Linus' defense team, which included young Hercules who testified that he had just reacted to Linus in order to protect himself from further abuse.

Although the argument convinced judges, it was less convincing to Amphitryon. Hercules' stepfather had discovered that the rapidly decreasing supply of tutors could be attributed less to ill luck than to his stepson's bad temper. Hercules was then removed from the highly-cultured curriculum and moved to a cattle station in the deep country, where any damage he may have would be minimal. Apollodorus, an ancient Greek writer, summarizes the story as follows:

Linus was Orpheus's brother. After he had received a blow from Linus, he went to Thebes where he became a Theban. However, he was killed by Heracles' lyre. After Linus had given him a blow, Heracles became furious and killed Linus. Heracles, being tried for murder, quoted Rhadamanthys law, which stated that anyone who defends himself against a wrongdoer shall be granted bail. He was therefore acquitted. Amphitryon sent Amphitryon to a cattle farm, in fear that he might do it again.

Apollodorus Library 2.4.9

The young man was now faced with a choice. He had done nothing in his life, except for the killing of a tutor or two. However, he already knew that his unnatural strength came from the Gods. Given the way strength was venerated by heroic Greece, his physical prowess was just as valuable as money in a bank. His solidly aristocratic heritage was not to be overlooked, as were the reports of his divine parental lineage. While he was not able to become king in Mycenae due to his lack of opportunities, Hercules became a successful cattle baron. This was possible only by being significantly stronger than the bulls that his herdsmen tend to.

The young Hercules should attempt to replicate, or even surpass, Perseus's great ancestor Perseus. They must also seek glory through danger and pain.

Or should he relax in pleasant indolence and (to quote an older poet) with 'Vacant hand and eye/Easy to live and quiet die'? Walter Scott's The Bride of Lammermoor.

The dilemma became physical for Hercules. Xenophon (the same man who, in 399 BC, led the march to the Ten

Thousand in one great adventure of Greek military history) tells the story. The story of 'Choice of Hercules' is told by the retired general in his memoirs.

He [Hercules] sat in silence and contemplated. He began to contemplate which path he should take and two women appeared. Both were tall and unnaturally big, but the woman in front was taller than the others. The one that he chose was beautiful and confident. Her limbs were strong and her eyes were clear. Austere was the name of her figure. Her robe was white.

The other was plump and soft after good meals. Makeup highlighted her natural pink and white features. Her clothing exaggerated and displayed her beauty, rather than hiding her talents. Doe-eyed, s/he admired herself and her shadow, before quickly looking around to see who might have noticed.

The first kept up her steady pace as she approached but the second pushed past, eager for her turn. "Heracles. I see that your considering which path to life you should follow. You can be my friend. Follow me, your journey will be easy and pleasant. You will never face hardship and all the joys of life will be yours. Let go of worries and wars. What you enjoy the most is your concern. The scent, touch, or fragrance that most delights you, the kind of tender love you are most attracted to, and which bed is most comfortable for you. You don't even have to put much effort in order to achieve these.

'You don't need to worry about not being able to afford your luxuries. Nor do you need fear that I will make you pay for them. Others will do the hard work for your, and they won't hold back anything. I give my permission to those who follow me to do whatever they wish.

Heracles listened to this and asked: "Please tell my Lady, what is you name?"

She said that her friends called me Happiness. My enemies call me Vice.

The other continued to speak. Now, she spoke too. "I also came for you, Hercules. I know your parents. I have also followed your education. It is my wish that you choose the path that leads me. You will make a difference and be an example of greatness and excellence. I will be honored and illustrious for my efforts. You will be a great and noble person, and I will make you more illustrious and honoured by my gifts.

The Gods have directed that nothing worthwhile is given to man unless he works to get it. To win the favors of the Gods you must worship them. You will only be able to love friends if you do the right things for them.

Vice said this to Vice: "You hear what this lady says, Heracles?" The road to joy can be long and hard. Let me help you find the short and easy road to happiness.

Virtue countered, "You poor creature." If you have not done anything to earn it, what good thing are you getting? You can't wait to have what you want, but you can get them before they are there. You eat before it is hungry, and you drink before it is thirsty. ... You live in wantonness by night, and you sleep poorly the best days of your life. You are immortal and the outcast among the Gods.

It is not the best thing to hear but praise, and you will never hear it. The sweetest sight you will ever see is the one that you do yourself. ... How can a man be sane enough to join your ranks? Your followers are young and weak. Their souls become void of foundation when they grow old. Although they seem young and fit, their souls become drained and worn as they reach old age. Past deeds bring shame, present deeds, distress. They were young, and they had to burn through their pleasure, but saved for their old age.

"My company is associated with Gods and great men. Without me, they can do nothing worth while. I am known by craftsmen as a loved workmate. I keep the home safe and protect the workers. ...'

"Come to the appointed time, my followers will not be forgotten or dishonoured. They live in song and memory for ever. Heracles is the son noble parents' Heracles. You will experience genuine happiness if you work in this manner.

Xenophon Memorabilia 2.1.21-34

Xenophon believes that all posterity is aware of which Lady Hercules they chose to follow. Contemporaries may not have been clear, but two events occurred in Hercules' 18th year. Amphitryon had settled in the areas east of Thebes. These lands were close to Thespis' kingdom. They also faced the Cythairon mountain range, which later formed the natural frontier between Athens/Thebes.

The mountains were steep, sinister, and Sophocles claimed that "no corner of Cythairon was echoless" in his play Oedipus. These dark, deep gorges gave birth to a great lion that fed on the Herds of Amphitryon as well as the flocks from Thespis. Many people were also victims to this relentless predator. Some were herdsmen and were killed with their cattle. Other nobles set out to hunt and feed the great beast. Euippus was the prince from Thebes who died. His death inspired Hercules. Hercules was actually in charge the cattle, right at the lions' main feeding grounds. The path of duty was the right one for the latest follower in Virtue.

Hunting the Cythairon mountain range was difficult. It is more then ten miles from the end to end and offers a variety of hiding places for large lions. Hercules needed to be closer to the mountains in order for him to embark on his expedition. This he achieved by taking up residence at Thespis the king. The kings of Thespis were more famous than young Hercules at this time, although he was only a lover and not fighter. Thespian king Thespian was a prodigious achiever in his field of endeavour. He had fifty girls of nubile ages. Perhaps because of his significant contribution to heroic Greece's population, the king had an interest in eugenics.

While the (alleged), son of Amphitryon wasn't known for much, other than his ambition to defeat a murderous animal lion, the young Hercules was still a remarkable sight. He stood four feet tall in his sandals and seemed small. Goliath was six feet tall when he was killed by David, five generations earlier. 45 cm is a cubit, which is a foot-and half. He was also a blonde, as it happened. This is revealed in Euripides from a short reference to Hercules' Lion-skin Helmet, which 'hided his yellow hair. (Euripides The Madness of Heracles. l.359)

Hercules and Thespis agreed that Hercules' elder daughter could be a companion at night after long days of hunting.

Hercules was eventually able to capture the lion. The story of the actual fight is still unknown. While it is possible that the hand-tossing was intense, it does not mean that the event was. Hercules was not only skilled at close quarters fighting, but also had an exceptional skill as an archer and a dab hand using a javelin. It is most likely that Hercules executed the deed with the blunt tool which was his trademark.

Our hero was able to hunt Mt Helicon, one of the most distinguished peaks in Cythairon's range. Helicon was sacred to Muses. Hercules might have taken a dip in the Hippocrene water spring that gushes from the mountain flanks. It had been struck by the hooves and wings of the winged horse Pegasus. Hercules discovered an olive tree that was tough and gnarled with a unique hardness. He tore down the tree and turned it into a club.

This was the club that Hercules used to introduce himself as a villain and monster to his era's villains. The Thebans were so proud that their adopted son was immortalized on hoplite shields a thousand-years later. Although it is likely that the Cythaironlion was the club's first victim the story of that climatic portion of the lion hunt is lost. Overshadowed by a later revelation: that Hercules the king had not been totally honest with him.

Thespius was Thespius' king, and Hercules accompanied Him when he tried to kill the Lion. The king was his host for fifty consecutive days. Thespius sent one or more of his daughters to stay with him each night after Hercules returned home from the hunt. He was determined that his daughters would have children by Hercules. Hercules thought he was sleeping with the exact same girl, but in reality, he had sex every one of them.

Apollodorus Library, 2.4.10

This deception seems a little more plausible when you consider that Graeco Romans believed the tale, and even had nice girls do it without lights. Martial, a Roman imperial poet, wrote about a girlfriend who would do anything, wherever, so long her boyfriend could't see it happening. Hercules spent days trekking through the mountains, and then he had to give up on the idea of exploring further.

This statue of Thespius' young Hercules suggests the possibility that Thespius's daughters might have been open to his plan.

Roman statue of Hercules in Metropolitan Museum of Art, New York

The king was in fact successful beyond his wildest expectations. Hercules was so powerful that he took on the challenge and left behind fifty ex-girlfriends who were pregnant. These children formed the Heracleidae, the descendants (very many) of Hercules' who later swept across the Peloponnese ending the conflict between Pelopids/Perseids.

Later Greeks called it the 'thirteenth Labour of Hercules'. It involved the impregnation of fifty young girls, while simultaneously engaging in a grueling hunt for a monster leopard. Technically it was the zeroth labour. But, while there were plenty of greek nit-picking pedants, these people didn't understand the concept that zero is a number. The first feat had to be completed at the end. His feats in Cythairon, which were particularly impressive to Greeks of his day made Hercules a man to be admired by fathers of teenage daughters.

Our hero had reached his stride and showed no signs that he was slowing down. His second adventure brought him to Hercules. This was even before he had returned home. He encountered Orchomenus ambassadors just before Thebes gates.

Orchomenus at that time was the most powerful and important city in the area, where the Minyans lived. The Minyans are an ancient people that pre-dates the more recent stock, among which Alcmene was numbered and Thebans were also numbered. Archaeologists suggested that there may have been a connection between the Minyans, and the Minoans. The Minoan civilization dominated the seafaring states of bronze-age Aegean. Orchomenus might have had very close connections with the powerful Minoan civilization, even though it was not actually a Minoan settlement.

The Minyans were certainly not a people to offend. But that was precisely what the Thebans had done. A Theban car, driving at high speed near the temple Poseidon, had thrown a large stone that had struck and killed a Minyan king. Orchomenus demanded payment of a hecatomb each year of cattle for twenty years in recompense. (A hecatomb was the standard unit for cattle and 120 of them were considered to be a hecatomb.

Hercules was himself a rancher, so he inquired lightly if a "hecatomb" was excessive for such a small place as Thebes. The ambassadors replied in arrogance that the hecatomb represented their city's extraordinary restraint. Properly, they should not have taken just the cattle but also the noses or ears of Thebans.

This was the wrong solution to give a confident and powerful young man who was Theban by adoption. The ambassadors left Orchomenus without their noses or ears, and were strung around their necks. Hercules also removed the ambassadors from their hands in order to prevent them from removing these horrible garlands. Then, he informed the victims that this was all their tribute from Thebes that same year.

Three sanctuaries can be found along the road to the Neistan gates. The closest sanctuary to the Neistan Gate is Heracles. It's located in an open field. Hercules, here, is known as 'the nose trimmer'. The Thebans explain that Hercules cuts off the noses heralds from Orkhomenos in order to collect the tribute.

Pausanias' Guide to Greece 9. 25. 4

Orchomenus's retaliation was unavoidably swift and indignant. A host of chariots stormed the city demanding the surrender of the impudent youths who had mutilated the ambassadors. Creon, Theban King, felt he could not resist following orders. The Minyans invaded Creon's home and killed not one but a few

Theban kings. The Minyans had also taken the armour, weapons and armor of the Thebans to keep them subservient. Creon must have thought that if his city couldn't withstand Minyans before (when they were properly armed), what chance did his people now that they were almost defenseless? So he sent men out to locate Hercules to hand him over the city's oppressors. Now it was nightfall and the young hero wasn't anywhere to be found. He was already out of town, further cementing his legend.

Chapter 3: Triumph And Madness

Hercules was more specific in his actions, as he sabotaged the Orchomenan horse chariot horses. He also gained an additional name that would be with him through antiquity, Hippodetus. It was early Greece, as well as the entire ancient world that had no idea of animal rights. Hercules was seen sneaking into the corral with the enemy horses at night and making the chariots useless, hamstringing those horses who pulled them. This was an intelligent ploy without any unpleasant side-effects. The Minyans without their feared Chariots were little more than a small band of infantry equipped with unsuitable weapons.

The Minyans, however, had weapons. This is more than the Thebans could say. Hercules, however, had also considered that. His latest exploit was reported in the news, and the young men protested the peace of King Creon. They demanded to be led away from their oppressors.

Hercules said to them: "Go to temples," and there take the arms and armour of the past generations.

This might have caused some degree of uncertainty among the war-like and hot-headed young men. These weapons were considered sacred by the Gods. This was because warriors who had accomplished great feats in war would surrender their arms in exchange for the God's favor. Also, the Olympian gods owned the weapons that were kept in the temples.

Given that war with Orchomenus would be a poor business venture at best and would it not be smart to start off by alienating Gods whose support the city needed to survive?

The time Hercules required the support and guidance of his divine father was in this very early stage of his career. Hercules would be nothing without the sign that Thebes was favoured by the Gods. They were happy for their armour being used in the cause of the city. Zeus was there to defend his son. The Gods gave their consent to the Thebans arming by arming themselves, as demonstrated by the fact Hercules was armoured by the Gods. The Gods provided the hero's with the most amazing array of arms and weapons in the young world.

The armour was so amazing, and so clearly of divine origin, that Thebes' would be warriors fled from their reservations to seek out temples to re-arm themselves with the best.

The writer must give up the page to Hesiod at this point. Hesiod wrote these events in eighth-century BC. Hercules will soon don his divine armor and lead the rag-tag army to battle. Hercules was just like any other self-respecting fighter of his day and as the Greeks were to do two generations later before the walls of Troy, he was going to war in a chariot. His chariot driver is addressed by him.

'Iolaus. The rough battle has come to an end. Do now what you've done so skillfully before. Help me as best you can to turn Arion our great black-maned pony, fast in every direction.

Hesiod: The Shield of Heracles

Iolaus, Hercules' halfbrother Iphicles, was named the chariot driver. It is therefore a mystery why this name is being used. Iphicles was just six years old when he had his first child. It would not be prudent to give such an infant control of an instrument of warfare that was, in the ancient world's eyes, something between a battle truck and a sports car. Arion was one of the horses.

Arion is the first-mentioned Hercules' set divine weaponry. This is because Arion was no ordinary horse, and it was difficult for amateurs to control him. Black-maned Arion, the child two Gods Poseidon and Demeter, was born. Legend says that Poseidon the Lord of Sea was captured by an incestuous love for Demeter, the Goddess of the Corn, and earth-shaking Poseidon. Demeter tried to escape her brother's gaze by becoming a mare and hiding in a pack of horses. This was a stupid choice. Poseidon is also God on Horses. He quickly located the beast, which was not his. Demeter was quickly converted to a horseman and he mounted her before she could flee. Arion was the result of this forced union.

Bronze age chariot with driver

Detail of a contemporary vase found in the Metropolitan Museum of Art New York

(Some academics believe that such a myth may have its origins in an earthquake-induced tsunami [Poseidon] which flooded a cornfield with [Demeter]. After being salted by seawater the land was used to produce horses [Arion]. These mundane explanations should be ignored and Arion's prodigious size and strength should be celebrated.

He is defeated by the east and west wind. He also carries Amphitryon's son in arms, fighting fiercely with him and demanding control.

Statius, a Roman poet, stated so (Thebaid 6). Arion was clearly not My Little Pony as a six year-old Iolaus. You might be better to believe that Iolaus, son Iphicles was named in honour this charioteer that served Hercules so well that day.

Heracles placed greaves in shining bronze on his legs. These were Hephaestus's wonderful gift.

Hesiod.122 ibid

Greaves were a kind of footless, rigid, metal sock worn at the ankle and knee.

The giant Greek battle shield protected everything between knee and throat. However, Achilles discovered that protection for the lower extremities of the body was also possible with this huge shield. Some warriors wore the single greave on the leg that was pushed forward in battle-line. Hercules, however, could afford a full set. Hephaestus the Craftsman God Olympus made his. Hephaestus is known for making the finest armour in the heavens and earth. It is also a good thing Hephaestus didn't speak to his mother. Hephaestus being Hera's child, it is not surprising that she was bete noir armoured herself by her own offspring. This probably did little to improve the relationship between child and parent.

Next, Hercules fastened a cunningly designed golden breastplate. This was Pallas Athena's gift. The powerful warrior placed his armour that protects people from death on his shoulders. He then threw his hollow quiver over the back. There were many death-dealing, arrows within. The shafts were long and smooth. At the end they fletched like the feathers of an eagle. He grabbed his powerful spear with its point made of shining silver. His heroic head was supported by a well-made helmet, made of diamond-hard. This helm fitted his temples closely and protected his godlike brow.

Ibid., l.125ff

Apollodorus, second-century BC writer, states that the bow was given to Apollo by Apollo. He also mentions that Hercules had a sword from Hermes, which was meant to complement his olive-tree club shield and magnificent shield.

He reached for his shimmering shield which was held by none of them. It was beautiful, glowing with shiny gold and shimmering with white ivory, enamel and electrum... deadly Fate was shown holding one man unwounded and one man with new injuries. One of her victims was dead. She was still dragging her feet along the chaos. She carried a reddish human blood garment on her shoulders. Terrifyingly, she glared at her teeth and groaned.

l.139ff. Ibid

The shields of legendary heroes are described in a whole sub-genre of classical poetry. Achilles had one, Aeneas the other - these shields are not just artifacts that carry symbolism, but massive works of art. In order to contain all of the subjects, each shield needed to be large enough for a roof to support a substantial building. One of the many scenes that Hercules' shield depicted in great detail included battle scenes as well as sporting and other scenes.

Perseus the horseman was also present. The son of Danae with a rich hair, he had winged sandals under his feet and a black-sheathed knife hanging from his shoulders. He flew as fast as he could, with the head and the Gorgon on his broad shoulders in a bag full of silver, which was amazing to see. There were bright tassels of golden from the bag. The terrible cap of Hades, which was dark as the darkest nights, was worn on the head by the hero.

l.216ff. Ibid

The shield displayed the world Hercules in all its forms, including its people at war, work, and play. The shield represented the world that Hercules lived in.

Ocean, the full stream that surrounded the shield and surrounded it, flowed around the rim. Here swans sang and called, while others were swimming in the water with shoals upon fish. It was incredible to look at the massive, strong shield. Even Hephaestus, the loud-thundering Zeus who had ordered it to be made and fitted, found it amazing. Zeus' valiant son wore the shield so well that he was as agile as lightning and leapt onto his chariot.

L.314ff.

After the long descriptions of Hercules, in all his martial glory, the actual campaign to defeat the Minyans are usually dismissed in a few sentences. This is as if Hercules main achievement in this short war was to dress for it.

According to myth, Thebes was near an ancient lake. The hero Cadmus established the city after killing a water dragon that protected it. The classic Greeks did not know of such a lake. Modern geology proved this to be true.

The Minyan king arrived at Thebes in his army. His arrival was met by Hercules' Theban minute-men "at a narrow location". (Diodorus Siculus 40.5). This was probably somewhere between the mountains and the lake. The Thebans were helped by the battlefield's constrained nature, much like the field of Thermopylae was for the 300 Spartans. The enemy host may have been huge but its soldiers were obliged to line up in an orderly manner to enter the battle. There wasn't enough space for everyone to go at once. After reaching the front line,

Hercules' wrath met the Minyan soldiers and they were quickly mowed down.

The battle was more evenly fought in areas not dominated Hercules. Most accounts agree that it was here while maintaining the Theban battlefield-line in place that Amphitryon, stepfather to Hercules, died heroically while fighting. It was a tragic loss that later tragic plays could not handle. So, they insist that he survived. After this battle, we should consider Amphitryon being a lot like Schroedinger's cat.

Amphitryon lost in the battle and poetic justice demanded that the other side also die. Poetry is very powerful when told through poets. So in those stories in which Amphitryon eats the dust ('bite the dust' being a quotation from Homer's Iliad. Book 2, line 369) then the Minyans king must also die. The Minyan king survives in the stories where Amphitryon is killed, but he remains captive to the victorious Thebans. The Minyan ruler made peace with Hercules. The tribute which had caused the war was now halved. But, it was due by Thebes to the Minyans.

In the grimmer version, the Minyan ruler and his army were murdered and Hercules' men benefited from the weapons and armour of their slain. As the sun set, they arrived at Orchomenus looking more victorious than they really were. The Minyans assumed, but misunderstoodly, that this was an army they had returned from defeating the impertinent Thebans. They allowed the soldiers to enter the city trustingly. In this version, the Minyans do not pay any tributes to the Thebans at end of war because once Hercules was done with their city and his men, there were no Minyans and no Orchomenus left to pay anything.

As word spread about the killing of Cythairon's lion, there was another account of Hercules feats as a great general. Armed and armored by the Gods. The young hero who had humbled Orchomenus.

Hercules was now one of the most respected warriors of his age, and the king of Thebes could be proud to have him as his son. Hercules was made a prince in Thebes by the marriage of Megara, his oldest daughter.

Megara's name is disputed. It was named for a Greek Greek city north-east and Athens. Megara or the legendary character? The bride was probably named after the city. Megara has been settled in the area since very early times.

The bride was named Megara, regardless of how she got it. Our hero temporarily quit his job of slaughter to become a husband/father. The couple settled down in the home Alcmene, who was still happily married to Alcmene.

It is unclear how long this period was of domestic bliss. The varying accounts of the number born into the family can be used to estimate the duration. This interlude in serenity lasted anywhere from five to ten years, depending on the poet who was counting.

Accounts of what happened after the fact vary despite the differences in the Hercules' children. Once again, we must agree with the general consensus. We also need to note outliers, such as Euripides' radically different version of the playwright. But then scriptwriters are not supposed to compromise the truth of the story.

Everyone agrees that Hera's malice ended the spellof herculean bliss. She was not able to forget her feuding with the son of her husband's illicit affair. Her ability to carry out a decent vendetta was constantly questioned by that man's continued well being. Zeus was happy at the moment with Hercules. Hera therefore had to subvert Hercules' mighty protector to make Hercules' lives miserable.

Megara, Hercules & child

Adapted using the Asteas Vase, 4th century (Museo Arqueologico Nacional Madrid).

Hera made the point that, in the initial years after the birth of the world, it was quite chaotic. The mythical world of Greek myth did not come into existence through more organized versions of the creation. Instead, it was created spontaneously by a faber Deus (a term mythologists refer to as a 'Creator God). The mythical world came about by chance, as matter was formed from chaos. This was an entirely random process, and some of these creatures were very powerful, extremely destructive, and downright antisocial.

However, the monsters that were capable of devastating the cosmos Zeus and his comrades had been defeated - although not without difficulty. However, this left many monsters running the world of mythology. They were able to cause havoc regardless of the best efforts of the current group of heroes. Their numbers are shrinking because of the inherent dangers of the job. (Even the apparently unkillable Cauneus was to perish in battle. Instead, a demented centaur used his tree-trunk as an axe to nab him.

Zeus wasn't responsible for creating the Earth. He and his brothers had split the cosmos among them, with Poseidon occupying the sea and Hades the Underworld taking the heavens. Nobody could control the Earth, due to the fact that the Earth was a powerful goddess in itself - Gaia the grandmother Zeus as well as all other Olympian gods.

Hera noted that Zeus' bad reputation was due to monsters ravaging grandma's place, which made Zeus look bad and disturbed many mortals who looked up to Zeus as protection. Zeus was fundamentally the God Order. That is why he commanded the government of Gods, men, and women. However, the Earth was looking very disorganized. Zeus did not do anything to fix this. His supposedly powerful son was also there, of whose potential Zeus had boasted so many times. What had the man done recently? He was the one whose greatest labour these days was changing the diapers for his infant babes.

The King and Queen of the Gods understood that his wife had a point. He was prepared to summon Hercules back into his heroic duties. Hera's diabolical plan was not complete with Zeus persuading Hercules to go back to work. It was an uncanny coincidence that Hercules received a summons right at that moment from Eurystheus the King of Mycenae. Mycenae being the dominant power within the region, Hercules could call on heroes like Hercules in an emergency. Eurystheus decided that heroism was possible, just as Hera was working on Zeus.

Eurystheus, suspicious of Heracles' growing power, summoned Hercules into his court in order to give him instructions.

Hercules ignored this command, until Zeus sent him an order from Eurystheus. Heracles traveled to Delphi to confirm this by speaking directly to the Gods. The oracle answered that it was the will the Gods that Heracles perform twelve Labours, under the supervision Eurystheus. If he could complete them, he would be immortalized. Heracles felt deeply disappointed by this development. He thought of all his accomplishments to date and felt that he did not merit to have his work monitored by someone he considered below him. However, he saw that he would hurt himself if Zeus did not follow him, who was also the father of his son.

Diodorus Siculus 4.10 -11.

Hercules was proud. In fact, this was one defining characteristic of the man. It is unknown whether Hercules knew that Eurystheus had succeeded him in assuming the Mycenaean Trinitary through an unfairly pre-born birth. But, Hercules was certain to have considered Eurystheus a Pelopid. Hercules felt it was demeaning to join the Peloponnese family's dominance, despite his noble ancestry via Pursues. He hesitated and failed to comply with the clear-cut orders of Gods, giving Hera an opportunity to strike a vicious blow.

His chronology is a bit suspect but Euripides, the playwright, gives the best account. Even as Hera planned on Mount Olympus and matters political were developing in Hercules' hometown of Thebes. While Hercules stayed at Delphi the king of Thebes fell to a usurper. Lycus, a child of Poseidon the Sea God, was the man who overtook Lycus. Lycus noticed that Megara (the wife of Hercues) had children of her very own. These children could claim the throne because they were the direct descendants of the former King. Lycus's power would be insecure unless the children and their mom were executed, as it was a matter of dynastic principal. (And Amphitryon also, this being one occasion when he was alive.

To ensure the executions were smooth, the usurper King decided to supervise them personally. Unfortunately, this was not wise. Hercules returned to Delphi just as an execution squad was getting ready for its final mission. The hero was shocked to see his family wearing funeral robes. He demanded to know the latest developments. His demands were hard to refuse, as Hercules are very demanding. The news update was quickly followed by Theban's shortest counter-revolution.

Megara's dad was restored to power by a happy populace. Lycus' remains were unceremoniously interred at Hercules' front door. Everything seemed to be fine, so the family settled down to a formal meal to remember their narrow escape. Unbeknownst of them, an invisibly uninvited guest was also present at the occasion. Lyssa, a deity that causes madness, was present. Hera ordered her to obey, and she reluctantly followed her orders.

I am Night, the beautiful daughter of Uranus' noble parents. I don't anger friends with my power, nor do I enjoy visiting the homes or houses of men. ... . This man against whose houses I am sent, is famous in heaven and Earth alike. I implore you not to wish him horrible harm.

I call the sungod to testify that I do not will do anything. If it is true that I have to serve Hera and be like the hounds who in full cry follow their huntsman, then I will. The ocean's murmuring waves and earthquake will not be as furious as my headlong charge to the heart of Heracles.

Euripides The Madness of Heracles (l.842ff).

The news was later carried to Thebes by a messenger who relayed the story to the shocked assembly.

'Sacrificial victim were placed in front of the altar to Zeus. The house was to be purified because Heracles had taken the [usurper] king from his hall and cast him out. His three beautiful children were standing together, along with Megara and her father [Amphitryon]; the basket was already being passed around to the altar, and they were keeping holy silence. Alcmene saw that his son was holding the torch in his right palm to dip into the holy waters. But he didn't say a word. His children looked up to see their father delay. Oh! He looked different. His bloodshot, bulging eyes were a stark contrast to his natural beauty.

"Eventually he spoke, all while making a demented chuckle. 'Father why should I give up before I have killed Eurystheus? Why would you light the purifying torch only to have it burn again? All those whom I have murdered will be purified as soon I bring in the Eurystheus' head. You can pour the water, and then toss out the baskets. Ha! You can now give me your bow! I'm headed to Mycenae. I'll need pickaxes and crowbars. And with those iron levers, those city-walls ...'. I'll lift from their very foundations.

"And off he went. Even though he didn't have a horse, he assumed he did. He mounted himself on a chair and used a whip for the 'horses' to make it seem as though he actually had one. The servants, bewildered, looked at each others and asked, 'Is our Master fooling around or has he gone mad?

He uttered threats against Eurystheus and his imagination eventually led him to Mycenae. His father grabbed him with his muscular arm and asked him: "My son. What are you doing?" What does this unusual behavior mean? What does this strange behavior mean?

Heracles imagining it was Eurystheus, Heracles pleaded for Eurystheus to touch his hand. He shoved the man aside, thinking he was about killing the sons Eurystheus. They raced around in wild panic. One of them burrowed himself in the skirts his distraught mother had given him, while another fled to the shadows beneath a pillar. A third fled like a bird to shelter under the altar.

The mother exclaimed, "What's the matter?" What does it mean for a father to slay his children? Heracles pursued his child, accompanied by his elderly stepfather and servants who cried aloud. Finally, confronting the child he shot him through both the heart and the head. The boy fell back, his last few breaths of life spraying blood all over the stone column. Heracles shouted for joy and boasted, "That's Eurystheus' brood dead at mine feet as atonement for the father's hate."

"Then he turned on the child who crouch at the altar's foot in an effort to escape unseen. The poor child ran to Heracles' feet, throwing himself on his knees. "Oh, I'm your son, your child. Eurystheus doesn't consider me his son. Don't kill us, father!

'Heracles frowned as a Gorgon, but the boy was too close for his baleful bowing. So he dragged his club down and struck the boy on its head. A blacksmith also hammers the iron. He quickly added another victim to his pair, after the first son was caught. The madman grabbed his second son, and he ran to add another victim. But the poor mother grabbed her child before he could. The madman then, acting as if he were actually at the Cyclopean Walls [of Mycenae], crowbars opened the doors and throws away the door-posts. He kills both his spouse and child with one bad bow-shot.

Chapter 4: Hercules At Work

The archaic Greece world was more strict than the more forgiving modern era in that it took personal responsibility. Any modern court would quickly exonerate Hercules in the case of murder and infanticide by simply looking at the charge sheets. We also have the confessions of Lyssa & Hera, the real perpetrators. However, even then, impartial eyewitnesses quickly realized that Hercules wasn't insane at the time he did the terrible deed. His modern perspective was clear that he was innocent, but these excuses did not let him off the hook.

These standards were straightforward. Hercules did the same thing, so Hercules is guilty. Blameless, but guilty. Oedipus would do the exact same thing a generation later. He would admit that he had killed the father of his family and had slept with his mother, even though he had tried hard to stop those deeds. You can see the point. In an age of poor forensic tools, it was very easy for criminals to shift responsibility to the malign god.

Additionally, homicidal tendencies weren't acceptable outside of combat or during heroic everyday activity. A slayer who was clearly and irredeemably deranged may not be guilty but must still be taken down for the safety and well-being of the community. Irredeemably deranged is the key phrase here. Hercules' fate would be determined by his reactions when he regained consciousness.

Euripides reprises the tale with Amphitryon fully aware of the danger that Hercules might still be homicidally crazy when he comes to. Amphitryon also knew this: Hercules could be homicidally insane if this is the case. He warns mourners.

Be gentle with your old friends. If he does not, he may wake up and break his chains to destroy the house. My elderly friends, run! Escape his waking fury. Soon, as he runs wild through Thebes streets, he'll pile on more corpses to those who have already been killed.

Euripides: The Madness of Heracles. l.1055ff

His audience cheered his awakening and Hercules took full control of his faculties. It was now time to update him on the events of his madness. Hercules, a child in his era immediately recognized his guilt.

Alas! What is the point of me sacrificing my own life to save those of my precious children? Perhaps I should run and jump off a cliff. Maybe I should avenge the blood of my children by driving my sword through my own body. I'll at least get rid of the infamy and shame that might otherwise befall my life.

...Now, my dearest friends will be seeing me exposed the pollution incurred from my children's murder. What am I to do? Is there any way to escape my misery? Are you going to let me fly [off a rock] or just sink under the earth? I am so embarrassed by the evil that I have done. Please allow me now to hide my head in darkness of death. I have new blood-guilt and do not wish to inflict any harm on innocent people.

...Why should I live? What is the use of a life filled with misery and death? No! Let gorgeous Hera dance in bliss! Zeus' fiancee, Lethera, should dance on Olympus in her beautiful slipper! She has achieved her goal! She has taken me down to my core, right to the foundations. What man would want to pray to such gods? In jealousy of her husband's visit on the bed with a mortal woman, she decided to destroy a good man who has done nothing except good for humanity.

Euripides The Madness of Heracles - l.1055 - 1200 passim

There are several accounts of what happened next. The Thebans could not kill their hero, as he was evidently cured of his insanity.

Hercules, however, was disowned for his guilt. According to some stories Hercules remained home and was cared for by his parents during his depression. Some texts indicate that Hercules believed that the gallant man endures all the pains of the world and that this was the point at which he accepted the motto that "The gallant person endures all the pains of the world without fear." Recognizing his guilt, he fled Thebes and his place of ill-memory and sought exile in Athens. He was guilty of a terrible crime, and only great deeds were able to cleanse his soul. Delphi encouraged Hercules to return to Mycenae again, where he was placed in the service Eurystheus.

Some sources state that the Heracles name was given to our hero only after this time. The Delphic oracle explained to him that extinguishing Hera's malice would bring great glory. This would be Hera's glory, meaning that Hera's victim would live in legend forever and have a place in the Heavens. He would not destroy Hercules like he had intended. His name would clearly show that Hera herself was the legendary hero Hercules would be.

This idea appealed Hercules.

It was difficult fighting with a goddess. However, the oracle had shown Hercules that it was possible. He would be famed, if not glorious, and the entire world would know that it had been Hera who had brought him such immense success.

While the evil deed Hera incited cannot be undone, it can be made to backfire against its perpetrator. Hercules, the child murderer, would humblely place himself under Eurystheus' power, just as the Gods had decreed. By the deeds he would do, Hercules would expiate the crime in such a way that the world would still remember his name, even though Hera's name was forgotten.

The Labours of Hercules are an act of revenge.

Eurystheus

Father Zeus, Lord the Lightning, my heart has swelled with news. A beautiful baby has been born this day. He is Eurystheus ("Broad strength"), the son of Sthenelus and Perseus. He comes from your line. It is right that he will be the ruler of the Greeks.

Hera and Zeus; Homer Iliad 19.122.

Eurystheus is the king Mycenae

Taken from a 5th-century red-figure vase currently in the Louvre, Paris.

The kings of Mycenae were not happy men. The crown makes a head feel uneasy. It was doubly so in this case because the wearer was well aware that it should have been Hercules beneath it. Eurystheus wasn't easy to please, as he was a Pelopid in a country that still supports the Perseids. Eurystheus had been disturbed by Hercules' rise in fame. Even more disquiet was caused when he saw the manner of his rise. If Hercules can lead the defenseless, disarmed Thebans into a crushing victory over Orchomenus, then what will he do after he has been properly set up and is ready to seize Eurystheus's throne?

Eurystheus had a similar antipathy to Hercules because he despised and loathed him. Hercules was, in fact, being more than a little hypocritical. He loudly spoke out about his misfortune as the blameless child of Alcmenese and Zeus. Hercules, though he denounced Hera because he hated him due to his birth, also hated Eurystheus precisely for the same reason. Eurystheus, who was two months early, did not choose to be born when or with whom he was.

The proclamation of Zeus and Eurystheus made Eurystheus the king and queen of Mycenae. It was not something Hercules liked. He didn't choose his role, and was only a player in a much bigger game than himself. Eurystheus, despite no wrongdoing, was made the victim by the machinations others. He was a highly powerful, vindictive, homicidal, hero. Eurystheus noted that Hercules was not just a victim in this story. He also had a claim to the title. Alcmene was able to understand his reasoning much later.

This feud was not initiated by me. I am certainly your cousin and kinsman. This affliction came on because of the divine power and Hera. I didn't accept to be his enemy, but I had to join this struggle.

Naturally, I wanted to invent trouble in abundance. My midnight planning paid off as I learned how push aside and conquer my enemies. Yes, I had learnt to put aside my fears about the future. The son of yours was no nobody, but a true man. Yes, he did indeed become my enemy. But, I will still be kind to him, for he was truly a man worth his weight.

Eurystheus in The Heracleidae of Euripides. L.986ff

Hercules was soon on his way, to join Eurystheus. Hera was not required to highlight the king's benefits if his great rival died while he was performing his duties. Eurystheus was now more secure than ever on his throne. He didn't even have to fear that Hercules would come and do the deed in his madness that he had imagined.

According to the oracle, Hercules was required to complete ten tasks on behalf of Eurystheus. You can imagine that these tasks required some nightly scheming. We can see certain similarities in the Labours of Hercules as we read the chapters. One of these points is the fact that Eurystheus gained nothing from the tasks. This is something you should think about. Eurystheus chose Hercules instead of using him as his personal battering-ram against the armies or cities of his foes. Or, you could send Hercules to collect rare spices or precious stones to stock his treasury. Eurystheus, however, did not set such tasks. The Labours for Hercules weren't of any benefit to humanity.

This tells us something important about Eurystheus. He was the supervisor and arbiter of Labours of Hercules. The nature of these tasks was difficult. It was almost impossible. The task would have to be difficult enough to achieve the Delphi standard, which Hercules had sought in his vengeful quest after immortal glory.

Eurystheus, at the same time, had already kept a careful eye on the past and a time when Hercules could complete his missions. Eurystheus ceased to be a necessity for Hercules and his plans. Only way to stop his ex-servant from executing him quickly is if he can argue that he has performed the duty he was assigned honestly, impartially and without personal gain. This argument might not impress Hercules but it will work in court of public opinion. Hercules did the Labours because he wanted to increase his public image. However, if Hercules unfairly murdered the judge who was only doing what Delphi and the Gods ordered, it would only diminish the hero's glory. Eurystheus had no personal gain.

There is also evidence of a geographical progression to Labours. Because Eurystheus, the kingdom's monstrous nature was not suited to a herculean approach, the first six were all located in the Peloponnese. After these issues had been resolved, Eurystheus devised missions for Hercules that would take him away from Mycenae and away from Greece to reach the outer edges of the world. It was possible for Hercules to encounter something lethal in his travels. The execution of each mission also became an end. That's because it took Hercules as far from Eurystheus, for as long as was humanly possible.

Each Labour should do another thing: it should either directly or inadvertently put Hercules in contact with one of the most frightening creatures in the world of myth. (And there were many of them. Further reflection reveals that Eurystheus shifted this thought in a new direction. It was based upon the fact that Mount Olympus is home to some the most fearsome creatures known.

Hercules was not known as a diplomat or tactful. Hera already had a hatred for Hercules. It might be possible to assign tasks that would allow Hercules upset other Gods, and increase the anti-Hercules faith. This required some night-scheming as the task was obviously designed to offend Gods (e.g. "Go and punch Apollo across the nose," would have a negative impact on the task-setter more than the executor.

The task needed was one that could be done without divine displeasure and was executed with subtlety. If Hercules were to use the brute force, madbull-at the-gate style, it might be pointed out by a wrathful god not that the task was wrong, but how it was executed. Eurystheus might be suspicious if all Hercules' Labours were designed to upset anyone powerful or divine. The Labours did not provoke the wrath from any deity, but at least four of them were.

The Nemean Lion was the first Labour

The warm-up task was used as the opening task for the 10 assigned. Hercules only had to kill a monstrous, lioness and bring the pelt over to Eurystheus. Hercules would have to deal with these fearsome creatures during later labours. One example is that Hercules fought and killed Thanatos, Death's son, at one point. That task was not part of the mission specification. Dealing with a maneating lion was actually a gentle warmup for the Labours. This was not surprising considering Hercules' track record in that area, as the Cythairon mountain residents could testify.

While this particular lion was certainly a step above Hercules earlier efforts, it was nevertheless impressive. The beast wasn't a regular carnivore. Instead, it was a child Typhon had and Echidna. For the Lion to be understood, it is important that we briefly introduce our parents. Typhon was one the proto-monsters who nearly destroyed the cosmos. He was said to be 'half as tall as the stars', and had a hundred heads of dragons where the normal human brain would be. Zeus had attempted to fight Typhon face-to-face, but was soundly defeated. Team Olympus almost lost this battle, even though Typhon was finally under control with the combined efforts of all Gods. Although Typhon's threat had been contained in the end, all children of the supermonster deserved more that a token of respect.

Echidna is known as Echidna's mother. With such a title, Hesiod does the job better.

Ferocious Echidna the Goddess. Half a nymph, half a snake with speckled flesh and fair cheeks. She lives in the sacred earth and eats the raw flesh of the rock. She is far removed from the immortal Gods, and she has this magnificent home. Arima guards beneath the Earth. Grim Echidna the nymph, who is neither old nor dying throughout all of her lives.

Hesiod Theogony 295–305

Echnida, the lion-child of Typhon, was suckled, and then raised on the moon. After falling from Selene's bosom, he made his home in Nemea (in the Peloponnese), not far from Mycenae. The fame of Nemea's games was later earned by the Pythian, Delphic, Olympic Games and for the temple of Zeus, which is still part of it today, as well as for its Lion.

It was remarkable that the Argolid area, which included Nemea and other areas, would be affected by this monster. The Argolid was protected by Hera. However, Hera unleashed that Lion on those she was meant for to defend. One theory suggests that Hera preferred to bathe in sacred springs near Argos each year. This would have the effect of renewing her virginity, making her more attractive to her spouse. Hera believed she had been spied on while on a recent bathing excursion. She reacted violently.

Zeus's wife, Zeus, was quick-tempered and let him [the Nemean Lion] roam free to cause damage to Argos.

Callimachus Aetia Fragment 55

Like its Cytheronian cousin, the Lion set about depopulating all the herds and flocks in the area. The Lion was known for abducting and murdering young women. Each woman would be saved by local heroes, but the Lion would still lurk in the cave presuming it was its victim.

The Lion would turn back to its original form when the heroes came within his reach. The Lion served as both a punishment and a means of vengeance to Nemea's people. Delegations travelled to Eurystheus with the intention of pointing out how taxpayers expect action from their ruler in this matter. This is why Eurystheus made it a priority to get rid of the Lion. This is what was most surprising about the story: Hera permitted him to do it.

Eurystheus had been working hand-in-glove with Hera, so it's unlikely that Hercules would have Hercules execute this Lion. It is possible that Hera had given consent. Although it was one thing for a monster to be unleashed on the countryside in a fit pique, it was quite different for it to continue to destroy the land and make its protectors look bad.

Perhaps the Lion should now go, since those protectors were King Eurystheus as well as patron goddess Hera. It was possible that Hercules might not fall at first hurdle. However, Hercules may end up being defeated by the Lion. In fact, that was the beauty in this first Labour. Eurystheus would win over Hera no matter how things turn out. Perfect outcome would be for one antagonist to be killed while the other is mortally wounded. While unlikely, there are always possibilities.

So Hercules was sent off. Hercules only traveled for a few days to Nemea in comparison to later missions, which took him all over the known world. His destination was in the mountains nearby, a narrow pass with cave on the side.

Tretos, or 'Pierced' is the name for this pass. It is narrow as the mountains press in close to all sides... The cave of the famous Lion can be found here in the mountains, about 15 stades [2.3km] from Nemea.

Pausanias Guides To Greece 2. 15. 2

You can find out what happened next by Hercules. He told it to Phyleus. Theocritus, the poet, preserved the tale and recorded it in his bucolic Idylls (35.232ff) in third century BC.

Phyleus and Hercules

"An Achaean, who came from Archaea and Helix by sea," he said. He explained to me that he witnessed the slaying that creature, the monstrous, lion-like beast that plagues the countryside and is kept in its den by the grove dedicated to Zeus. The Argive did the killing. I believe that it was you. The lion skin covering your sides proves that you are responsible for this incredible deed.

'I'm sure such a massive monster wouldn't be found in Apis which supports only bears, boars, and I am certain it would. Tell the tale of how this terrible disease reached Nemea, and how your hands fought it.

Hercules and Phyleus:

'Since your ask, I can tell ya everything about this beast except from where it came. This is a matter of fact, none Argives know this - even if some make that claim. The best guess is that Phoroneus was an angry god with Phoroneus and his sons. Phoroneus was a primordial king in the Peloponnese who was, surprise, surprised, raped at the hands of Zeus. The scourge was unleashed like a river that burst into a canyon, it decimated all who were in its way. Bembiana had to endure more of this pitiless assault than they could handle, so Eurystheus handed me this first Labour. I had no choice but to kill this beast.

"So I set out taking my hollow quiver and my supple bow with me, along with arrows. I took my bow with me when I arrived at the Lions' hunting grounds. I tied the string to the curved ends of the horns and aligned with my grief-bringing archers. It was now a matter of searching for the accursed creature and finding him before I found him. I was unable to see his tracks or hear his roar. But the terror that hung over the farmsteads was still palpable. Even though it was midday, no man had plowed the fields or worked with his oxen. No one could even give me directions. I ran straight for the mountainside without pausing and searched. I would test my strength upon the Lion, once he was found.

'Immediately' didn't happen that day nor the next. Hercules searched vainly for weeks, believing that he was fated not to be where the Lion was. Despite the fact that the Lion was unaware of Hercules, time after time the whims or chance led him to the opposite side of the pass as

Hercules. After the Lion circled his hunting grounds, he would again enter and exit the pass through his cave, just like Hercules. The struggle continued for almost a whole month. Finally, the exhausted hero realized that this could go on forever. So, as his usual behavior, he took drastic measures in order to rectify the situation. The narrow mountain pass was gone in a matter of hours. The narrow mountain pass was closed by a Hercules induced rock-slide. Our hero was at the other end of the pass, hiding in the bushes with bow and gun in hand and a mind to kill. Hercules retells the story.

'It was late when the Lion returned from his lair. His tongue licked his chops after he had eaten meat, blood, and other things. You could see the evidence all over his pale, squalid face and his chest. I had been waiting in the shadow of some trees for him on that woodland path. As he passed me, I tried to hide in the shadows of some bushes and fired a quick arrow at his flank.

'I had expected the bow to pass between the ridges [of a lion's ribs], but instead, it bounced off and fell to the green grass. The Lion looked around, snarling in his teeth. Angrily annoyed at my first miss, I pulled out a second string. This time, the hit was right in the chest, just at the top of the lungs. The arrow that should have caused agony hit the hide but was instead dropped between his paws. I was furious and ready to draw the third one.

"But the rolling eyes from the monstrous creature had settled upon my, and I was prepared for battle. His tail bit his thighs, his throat was full of fury, while his hair was bristling with anger. In an attempt to taste my flesh, his spine bent like a bow and he pulled his length from his flanks to his midriff. In a flash, the terrifying creature appeared from afar and came upon me. I had just taken my cloak and folded it in half with the arrows in my one hand. I held in my other hand my seasoned club made of wild olive. I then swung my club back behind me and crashed it onto his skull. The invincible creature's skull was splintered by the hardened wood. But the brute fell before it could reach me. He fell and rocked on his feet.

I was shocked to see him so quickly that he couldn't regain his wits or his breath. I grabbed the beast by his iron neck, throwing my bow and embroidered quiver at the ground. I strangled him using all the strength in both my hands. He couldn't claw me so I did this from behind. My heels pressed his hind feet into the ground and my knees squeezed his flanks. The body was stretched out with my hands around the neck. Finally, the body collapsed under my arms. Hades, Lord over the Underworld, was then able to receive the Lion's spirit.

Hercules had triumphed. He had defeated the Lion, but his Labour was not over. Eurystheus would receive the skin of the great Lion. Hercules had a problem. His arrows bounced off a Lion's hide, because the Lion had two incredible attributes: claws that could rip apart anything (hence Hercules need to be careful) and an impenetrable cover. Hercules was now faced with a difficult dilemma. How can you remove the skin from a beast whose pelt is not easily removed? First Hercules tried to remove the pelt from the beast with a knife. This was just to confirm the results of the arrows. The blade made no impression so he tried sharpening the knife with a stone. Finally, he crushed the stone to sharpen the knife and attempted to cut the hide. Our hero was stumped when even that failed.

Hercules didn't work alone, but it was a blessing. Athena looked after her protégée as usual. Athena was clearly the brains of the outfit. The Goddess pointed out to the confused hero that an impenetrable cover could not co-exist within the same universe as claws that can rip through anything. Either the claws acted irresistibly or the hide was immovable. However, when the Lion's claws were applied at the Lions hide, something had gotta give.

Unbeatable Hero v. Invincible lion

This wine jug is black-figure and was found in Etruria c.510 BC.

The claws were the winner when the matter came up for trial. Hercules managed to cut the skin of the monster and take the pelt out. He took care when he did this. He remembered (or Athena more likely, it was the thought that Athena passed on the idea) Eurystheus had instructed that Hercules should bring the Lion's skin. This Hercules would be able to do. Eurystheus had the skin brought to him, so the Labour was done.

Hercules didn't intend to give it up after presenting the pelt to him for inspection. The hide was not just a trophy to celebrate the success of the first Labour. If the hide was properly removed from its former owner, it could be made into a coat. In light of the perils Hercules was facing, a garment completely impervious towards sharp objects was a welcome addition.

As Hercules concludes,

"There, my dear friend, is the tale of The Lion of Nemea's doom, the creature that caused so many sorrows to humans and flocks."

Theocritus Idylls 25.280

However, this is not the end of the story. Hercules was accompanied by Molorchus (a peasant farmer) on his way to face the Lion. Zeus Soter, Zeus the Saviour was planned by the farmer. Hercules convinced this man to stay for thirty days. To thank Zeus for his salvation, the couple would sacrifice to Zeus together if Hercules returned within that time. Molorchus, if Hercules does not return within the time period, will sacrifice again to Zeus, but this time to a spirit of the dead hero.

The sacrifice was already made and the ram was almost to be killed in Hercules's name when the honored guest arrived just in the right time. Although Zeus was honored with the sacrifice, Hercules had to organize a small funeral. Phyleus did not hear about the difficulties caused by pride or stoicism. The beast had somehow managed to take one of Hercules' fingers.

Heracles only had nine finger after the Nemean Lion had bitten of one. Sparta has a tomb to hold this detachable finger. To symbolise the power and might of the hero, there is a stone Lion placed on the tomb. So began the tradition to place stone lions on tombs of notable people.

Ptolemy Hephaestion. New History 2.

The Nemean Lion has a permanent memorial. This is fitting for such an enormous beast. As Leo's astrological sign, July to August, the Lion reigns over the cosmos. The constellation lies between Cancer and Virgo, in the eastern sky. Perhaps the Lion is dreaming of the distant future when slow galaxy drift will bring the constellation Hercules within his reach. In that case, they can face off in a celestial rematch.

Chapter 5: Hero At Work

Hercules presented itself at the court Eurystheus. There, he provided evidence that the king had successfully completed his first mission. The sight of Hercules in his lion-skin jacket, armed and invulnerable, brought a degree of reflection to the already fragile monarch. He decided that Hercules wouldn't have to present the grisly proofs of his crimes in person in the future. Eurystheus could resolve the issue by sitting in a group of judges outside the city gate without having to face his dangerous relative. Eurystheus ordered construction of a large-sized bronze urn in case Hercules did not follow the instructions. This was buried in the throneroom up to Hercules' neck, with a lid that could withstand severe pressure. Eurystheus sent

Eurystheus off again to complete his second mission.

Eurystheus' war with the children Typhon and snake-bodied Echidna was continued by this Labour. This time, the child in question followed after her mother. Echidna's lower half was that of a monstrous snake, but the Lernean Hydra did more and had not just the lower part of a serpent, but also the upper. The Hydra was not like the Nemean Lion, who plagued the Argolid even before the Labours were considered. It had been meticulously prepared for this challenge as a star athlete prior to a major event.

...the evil-minded Hydra von Lerna was fed white-armed Hera because the goddess was furious with her mighty Heracles.

Hesiod Theogony 333.

The Hydra was among the most lethally poisonous creatures created. Although smaller serpents can bite and kill, the Hydra can do it with her breath. Hyginus, the writer, tells us that the creature was so venomous that any man who even tried to breathe in while crossing the path where the monster slithered died in pain (Fabulae 31).

Locals were not surprised to be deeply disturbed by the monstrous creature's emergence. Although they were shocked, they were not shocked. Because the town was near a marsh it was already unhealthy. A lamb was offered to the Underworld, which was connected directly to the worlds men every year. In reality, Lerna was probably abandoned around the time the Hydra arrived - modern archaeological excavations at the site date it to the Bronze Age. Following that, the location was used as an Argos graveyard, possibly to save the deceased on their long journey to Hades.

It is only four miles from Argos that the sea at Lerna can be found. The Erasinus fountain, which flows into Phrixus and meets the sea between Temenium, Lerna, is the first place you will see on the road to Lerna.

Pausanias Guides to Greece 2.36.6

There was a hillock where the 'torpid water' from another spring left the marsh. Here grew a large oak tree. This spring was called Amymone and named after a distant relative of Hercules. Pausanias was the Roman Peripatetic, who saw the tree during preparation of his Guide from

Greece. However, by his time, there had been a bit of scepticism.

A plane tree is found at the source for the Amymone. It is believed that the Hydra developed its strength in the shadows of this tree. I believe this creature was more powerful than any other water-snakes. And its poison is extremely deadly. I do believe that it was originally one-headed. Peisander, of Kamiros, was the first person to describe it multi-headed. It did this in order to make the monster even more frightening and to make his poem more memorable.

Pausanias - Guide to Greece 2.37.4

This was where the Hydra's den could be found in the swamp. The Hydra's base was located under this tree in the swamp.

From there, it made regular visits to the surrounding area where it decimated crops as well as cattle herds. Eurystheus would again have been required to send a heroic figure to eliminate the creature, even if Hera was not planning on doing so. Hercules was familiar with this method of killing monsters as he did with the Nemean Lion. Seneca, the first century AD philosopher and playwright, said that Hercules was practising for Hydra when the serpents sent by Hera 'had their swollen necks crushed by his [Hercules] infant hands'. (Hercules Furens 220ff)

Pausanias may have also been correct in stating that the Hydra started out as the bane and savior of Argos. But Hera had created a surprise for Hercules, or any other hero who sought to destroy the Hydra. Hera organized that two heads would be created for every head. This was traditionally how a snake could be killed.

This is why Hydra became the symbol and name of the SLA terrorist organisation in the 1970s. If you take out one branch, two other branches will grow in its place. Today's 'hydraheaded' problem means that any solution will only make things worse.

The Hydra had nine heads at the time Hercules started to investigate it. This suggests that at least one hero tried to fight the beast. The Library of Apollodorus is the longest continuous account of Hercules meeting Hydra. This is where we now turn.

Eurystheus, in his second Labour, ordered Heracles kill the Lernean Hydra. The Lernean marsh-born monster would roam the plains and ravage both cattle and the country. The Hydra had nine heads and an enormous body. Eight of the nine heads were indestructible, while the middle was immortal. [Some reports claim the middle head was made out of gold]

Heracles then mounted his chariot with Iolaus as his charioteer and he made his way to Lerna. The horses were stopped when the Hydra was discovered at the hillside of the springs. Heracles unleashed fire arrows and forced the monster out of that den. Once it emerged, he grabbed it and held it tight.

Antonio del Pollaiolo (1431-1498) Ercole e l'Idra. Galleria degli Uffizi, Florence

The battle began. Hercules had secured himself against the snake's venomous breath with a wet scarf wrapped around his face. The Hydra reciprocated by wrapping its arms around Hercules. Here was another little surprise from Hera.

The Hydra was clinging to one of his feet as it wound around, but a large crab stepped in to help him by inserting its pincers under Heracles' feet.

Hercules broke the crab to pieces using his club, but the stubborn refusal of Hydra's heads to be stumped stopped him from continuing. Our hero continued to hunt down the beast and he did so until he was confronted by a forest of heads, each one dripping with its venom. The situation looked dire for our hero, until a flash of inspiration saved him.

The Hydra had already been helped by the crab. Iolaus, who lit a part of a nearby tree and heated his sword in flames, called the Hydra. Heracles began to remove each head. He then cauterized the stump, stopping new heads from growing. He then [Hercules] shaved off the immortal after having dealt with the multiplying head.

Apollodorus Library 2.5.2

Quintus Simernaeus, Roman poet, painted the scene in The Fall of Troy.

The terrible, long-necked Hydra flickered their terrible tongues. Although its fearsome heads were scattered on the ground, many more were sprouting from its necks. Hercules was a strong-hearted companion, while Iolaos was a more gentler one. The one who killed the monsters with his powerful strokes was the one who took down their fierce opponents. His companion rubbed every neck with glowing iron until he was done.

Many authors credit Athena with the brilliant idea of cauterizing Hydra's necks. Hesiod says bluntly, "by the plan and Athena" (Theogony 313). We do not know if Hercules cut the poison sac from the snake by implying it to the Goddess, or whether he was acting on his own initiative. The venom absorbed into the arrowheads, making them nearly as deadly as the snake. Even though it didn't kill Hercules, what did make him stronger was that he now had a deadly weapon to match the invulnerable shield made by the Nemean Lion. Hercules used to call his bows 'sorrow-bringing'. He didn't know how accurate this description would prove to be.

The last, immortal head had been the first to be chopped off. This Hercules was found buried by his driver on the road to Elaeus. He placed a large stone over the burial place to make sure it was not discovered. The remainder of his corpse was burned in the spontaneous pyre that the torchlight had set up. The marsh's waters were then hot, pungent, undrinkable. A sulphuric volcanic spring might be a possibility, given the marsh's link to the Underworld. However, the ancients had different ideas.

The marsh in Lerna where the heated heat of the burned Hydra makes the polluted waters warm

Statius, Thebaid 2.375

Death simply moved the Hydra over to the other side the Underworld portals. The monstrous snake was still there to guard the Kingdom from Hades. Cerberus, another well-known custodian and hound, shared this job. Although Hera sent the crab to be a footnote in this story, the creature was rewarded with a spot in the heavens near Leo for its kamikaze attack on the ankle. This made it the astrological sign Cancer.

The Cerynitian Hind

Hercules would have to count the Cerynitian Hid as Hercules second Labour. People with an arithmetical bent might not agree to this designation. As the Labours of the Nemean Lions, the Lernean

Hydra and the Lernean Hydra already made two Labours, the Hind should thus be counted the third. Eurystheus, however, ruled the Lernean Hydra a technical offence. This was because Hercules hadn't done the job on its own. Iolaus had been instrumental in the destruction of the Hydra's necks by cutting them off before other heads could grow. Eurystheus declared that The Labours of Hercules were not The Labours of Hercules Assistant.

We can now see the extent of Hercules' research into his quarry when a Labour was announced. Our hero would be well-served by investigating the history, strengths and weaknesses of the creatures he was facing. This is especially important for the next Labour. Hercules would discover that the Cerynitian Hind is unusual among female deer because it has antlers. These weren't normal antlers;

they were shining horns in the purest gold. The Hind was one in a group that included five deer. The Hind was one of five deer. (That is why Sir Francis Drake was England's great sailor during the Elizabethan period and called his ship The Golden Hind).

This super-deer was able to leap high buildings and run faster then a speeding arrow. Quintus Smyrnaeus, a Roman poet, wrote that this super-deer also caused problems in agriculture in Peloponnese. The late Roman poet Quintus Smyrnaeus said that the beast 'laid bare the vineyards of hapless spousemen... with its golden hair and breath of burning fire. (Fall Of Troy 6. 223) Callimachus, a poet, wrote seven hundred years before Quintus smyrnaeus that the Hind belonged to a group of deer (the third Hymn from Artemis 98ff).

Eurystheus, who had these characteristics, made it even more difficult to capture the animal. He also stipulated that the beast should not be hurt. It is surprising that Eurystheus had in mind to keep the Hind prisoner once it had been captured. It would be very dangerous to have the animal killed. This is where Hercules would have come in handy. Here is the summary.

It starts at Mt. Tagetus. The formidable mountain towers over Sparta in contemporary Greece. In ancient times, it was here that Spartans exposed their infant children to night terrors. Those who survived may have been assisted by Taygete the Nymph, a mountain denizen and mother of Lacedaemon the founder of Spartan. Taygete struggled with Zeus' sexual advances, as did many other nymphs. The King of the Gods refused to be denied was almost as perilous as his refusal to refuse his wife. Therefore, it is easy to understand Taygete's gratitude that Artemis helped her out of her difficult predicament. Artemis turned Taygete to a cow and Zeus turned his affections away. Tagete was then able to give five golden-horned elk to the Goddess as a thank you.

Five of them were there, and four of those you [Artemis] captured, all by foot speed, without the aid or assistance of hounds. They were assigned to draw your swift cart, and you did so to the golden chariot.

One deer however was too quick and ran over the river Celadon. Ceryneia gave her the... . (Callimachus ibid)

Artemis became fond of the deer that ran away, possibly because Pindar (522-243 BC) said that the hind actually belonged to Tagete. Artemis hunted with her deer companion Ceryneia, one of the twelve Achaean capital cities. It has a population today of five hundred.

Artemis would probably be annoyed if her deer was taken from them, but not if she was left with a companion who was hurt or even killed. Artemis shared the same traits as her twin brother Apollo. She had a large vindictive streak.

Leto, Leto's mother had problems giving birth to Apollo (and Artemis) as she was cursed with not being able to give birth on land and sea. She was also constantly denied a birthing place. The sacred island of Delos gave birth to the pair. Artemis and Apollo hunted and killed everyone who refused their mother shelter. Later Niobe the queen of Thebes claimed that she had fourteen kids while Leto only had 2. Leto's other two children were furious at Niobe's attitude and immediately took up their bows. They slaughtered all of the queen's children till she had left just one.

Chione, princesse de Phocis was killed for her prettier claims than Artemis. Adonis received the chop because he claimed he is a better hunter. Artemis apparently killed him by wild boars, and this is what the pork chop was. Actaeon the hunter was made into an animal and torn by his own dogs because he saw Artemis naked. Aura, goddesses of the breeze was raped, and driven insane for questioning Artemis virginity. Callisto was the late Orion, then there was Aura, goddess of the breeze.

Eurystheus' heroic order to Hercules capture Artemis' pet was quite admirable. And he was positively deranged that he believed he could keep the pet. The wily king was probably right to believe that Hercules would bear the brunt for the goddesses' fury. Hercules would be guilty, as Artemis' friend, of being the unwitting agent for Lyssa or Hera killing his children. Artemis and her contemporaries would agree that it would not matter who ordered Hercules, but rather what Hercules did. In the Heroic Age a man was held accountable for his actions.

As opposed to previous tasks that required the killing of dangerous creatures Hercules had to capture the dangerous and elusive creature alive. This was in order to avoid the more deadly Olympian Artemis. Our hero set off to Arcadia. He spent a year following the Hind through the mountains and valleys, while also learning the hundreds of ways he could not be captured. It was a beast that the Goddess of the Hunt failed to capture. Hercules' task was made more difficult by his desire to not hurt a single hair of the creature's beautiful hide.

The chase took people of Arcadia on a journey from Oinoe to Mt Artemision. They were entertained for weeks 'over mountain hideaways to untrodden pastures, through forests where flocks graze.' Aelian (Animalia 7.39) Artemision was Artemision's final refuge. Artemision later became a term that referred to any sanctuary for the goddess. It included the Ephesus temple, which was named one of the Seven Wonders of the World.

Hercules persistently pursued his quarry even as he fled. The Hind attempted the crossing of the Ladon River, which ran at the foot of the mountain and continued into the Ionian ocean.

Hercules Behind the Hind

Sketch of a Black vase 6th-century in the British Museum

Hercules was able to see his chance here, right at the spot where Demeter had washed away all the shame of having been raped for Poseidon. Although the river was not as deep as it seems, the rapid waters are shallower and the Hind struggled to cross. Hercules was a consummate archer and carefully chose an arrow to shoot at the Hind that was not contaminated by the Hydra's lethal poison. The arrow didn't go in the creature's mouth, but instead went between its front legs. This caused the animal to stumble into the waters, and according to some accounts, to damage one of its golden teeth. Hercules was at his prey in no time and quickly slung the captured beast on his shoulders before setting off for Mycenae.

Hercules met Artemis, a woman out for a walk, on the return trip home. Her equally vindictive twin brother Apollo was there to help her. Hercules had a few good points. Firstly, the Hind hadn't suffered permanent damage. Adonis (and Orion) could have testified to this, but Artemis, virgin or not, was always looking for a young man with a good body. Hercules was Athena's protege, and no-one could possibly offend Athena, regardless of whether they were a ploughman, or an Olympian god. Our hero used powers of oratory that he didn't even know he had and presented his case to Artemis. He blamed Eurystheus for the capture, and appealed in sympathy for the difficult circumstances that forced him to do the labours. Artemis and Hera were not a good couple, as is evident in a later incident.

Hera spoke as Artemis was speaking. Hera grabbed Artemis by the wrists, and then boxed her ears. Artemis attempted to twist away. Artemis' arrows flew [from her quiver] and were scattered. Artemis ran away in tears like a pigeon to ahawk.

Homer, Iliad 21.475

Artemis was not afraid to ruin the plans of Hercules' step-mother. She allowed Hercules to go, but only after he promised to return the Hind unharmed at the end of his Labour.

Heracles then soothed the goddess' wrath and brought the animal still breathing to Mycenae

Apollodorus Library 2.81

Hercules still had one problem. He had made promises to Eurystheus that the Hind would be delivered to his menagerie. Artemis, however, had promised Artemis that the Hind would be freed. Not delivering Eurystheus' Hind would have been the same as the death of the Hydra. Artemis had made a solemn promise that the Hind would be delivered as it was ordered. This prospect was not appealing, and Hercules probably spent the rest of his journey to Mycenae contemplating this conundrum.

As per protocol, Hercules was expected to produce proof that his Labours were completed to a panel made up of judges at city gates. Our hero claimed that he was not allowed to do so because of an order. He was instructed to deliver Eurystheus' Hind, and that no one except Eurystheus would be allowed to do so. The Labour would not complete until Eurystheus personally completed the delivery. Hercules made it clear that the Labour would be accepted despite technicalities. Eurystheus carefully accepted the terms as the Hind, which was quite innocuous in comparison to Hercules' usual quarry. Hercules presented the Hind ostensibly to the king upon his arrival at the city gates.

The Hind's famed speed was evident as soon Hercules released its grip. It quickly took off from a standing stand and briefly became a glowing streak, which disappeared in the direction Arcadia. Hercules was merely able to shrug it off, even though the royal court and courtiers were not impressed by this development. He had followed Eurystheus's orders to the letter and delivered Eurystheus his Hind. Eurystheus' incapacity to keep custody for more that a split-second was a problem. Hercules, however, had no problem. He had kept his promises both to

Eurystheus & Artemis. His Labour was complete.

The Origins of Greek Mythology

"The Titanomachy is a symbol of Order triumphing over Chaos." Niall Livingstone[1]

"The Greek Mythos could indicate, amongst various things, a public expression expressing the authority and speaker of the speaker."[2] Plato did not believe myths should be in the hands other than philosophers during the Classical Period. Myths help to define beliefs and create a way to observe and categorize patterns in daily life. Hesiod claimed that the "Pre-World," was populated [3] by personifications. Hesiod depicted the personifications he believed were primal elements and painted a picture of the primordial geopolitical geography of his worldview. This is a completely arbitrary folkloric trope. But in the case with the ancient Greeks the antagonism was infused by strains of uncomfortable duality. Hesiod had intended to honor Zeus. But he created a melodrama for the ages.

Marie-Lan Nguyen's photograph of Plato's bust

Hesiod uses the term "Chasm", a synonym for ancient Greek Chaos. The goddess Gaia is the mother-goddess Gaia. This was where the Tartara (or Tartarus) was found, and the Titans would be destined for their fate. Hesiod also mentions Eros (the embodiment of erotic Love) at the conception the cosmos, providing ancient Greek readers with a foundation in procreation and the lasciviousness for all deities. Thus, the act is created begins with Chaos, Gaia and Eros. But these are not benign personifications or grandparental figures. Chaos was capable without the need to have a partner in reproduction of the most macabre, inherently bleak, or "chaotic" elements.

The ancient Greek representation of Gaia holding Erichthonius, her baby, to Athena, as Hephaestus watches

The chaos spontaneously bore Erebus (Darkness), Nyx(Night), whose offspring were appropriately dark and should be credited accordingly to lessen the responsibility on Pandora for "bringing the whole of the sorrow into the universe." The Nyx-offspring list reads like a guest list with the worst traits of humanity: the Fates and Death Spirits, Apate (Deceit), Geras [Old Age], Ponus [Toil], Lethe (Forgetfulness], Limus [Famine], the Algaia] (Quarrels), the Pseudea Logii (Lies), Amphillogiae ("Disputes"), Dysnomia ("Lawlessness"), Ate" (Friendship), Ate "Delusion), Ate" (Del), Ate" (Friendship) and Horcus ("Oath) These peopleifications of darkness are the Titans' world inhabitants. The reader is immediately presented with a multitude of reasons why "order," should be respected and achieved at every cost in Hesiod's Theogony.

Gaia saw that Chaos didn't have any need for her and had to act as her own catalyst for cosmos. Gaia bore Ouranos Sky, whom Hesiod refers "Starry Heaven", so that "he should all about cover her" and "to be a secure place for ever for Gods." However, it wouldn't take long before Starry Heaven lost all connection with any "security" for gods.

Gaia and her firstborn son, Gaia, would be the most significant act in the early stages Greek cosmological history. But it also set up the foundation for the world where the ancient Greeks lived. From this visible union emerged the "insatiably bewildered" [4] Hecatoncheires ("the Hundred-Handed Giants") and the

Gigantes ("the Giants"), as well as the famed Cyclopes (the famous ones who built the great walls of Mycenae). These were the first and most powerful beings. They would play a pivotal role in the conflict between the Titans and gods. Hesiod envisioned a "Golden Age" where humans and divinities lived together on the same plane and interacted openly. This shows that even after two centuries with no major building, crumbling walls of ancient palaces still held the power to inspire theories of a divine history.

Johann Heinrich Wilhelm Tischbein's illustration of Polyphemus

The Titans' roles in early mythology were more complex than those of the first generation of Ouranos, Gaia's offspring and others who appeared out of Chaos. Kerenyi said that "these titans [are] a mysterious bunch; to suggest they were originally Nature-gods or ancestors is almost meaningless. The truth is that most of them are not nature-gods." [5] Hesiod gives Titans less ostensibly personified names, but gives them more complex personalities. With every successive level of power, one can see a progression from chaos into order.

Gaia, bedded with Heaven and Iapetos (Ouranos), was the mother of deep-swirling Oceanus. Koios were Kreios and Hyperion as well Hyperion and Iapetos. Thea and Rhea also had deep-swirling Oceanus, Koios. The youngest child was born to them after their deaths, the crooked schemer Chronos. This was the most fearsome of children who hated their lusty father. [6] This account is Hesiod's initial of the names for the first twelve Titans. "Deep, swirling Oceanus" refers specifically to the immense river that the Greeks believed was encircling their world. Mnemosyne would become the Titan of

"Memory" and go to bed with Zeus' nephew. She would also give birth to the Muses. They were beloved poets who inspired Hesiod. These names, aside from the Titans, are not personifications. Their actions and characters are more important than representing any universal force or element. The story is then rewritten with new protagonists as well as antagonists, particularly when it comes to Chronos, the "crooked planer".

Roman mosaic depicting Ouranos, Gaia and other characters

Hesiod refers the Titans to as "chthonic" They were "born out of the Earth", and their subsequent "imprisonment in her" defines them further. Ouranos hated children and made Gaia place them back inside her to keep them safe indefinitely. Ouranos didn't intend to stop his lust to Gaia, no doubt due to his primordial uncle Eros. He "enveloped" Gaia even while she was pregnant but would not allow "nature" to happen afterward. Hesiod's Theogony provides the first glimpse of an aberration in nature. It is here that a wicked dad overpowers a divine Mother.

Ouranos thought that all children who were born of Heaven and Earth were the most frightening of children. Even their own father was afraid of them. After each child was born, he kept them in a cavern on Earth and wouldn't let them out into the sunlight. He was happy with the wicked work, but the Earth was too big to breathe. She came up with a horrible trick. Without delay, she invented the grey adamant element, created a great reaping catch, and then spoke to her children to encourage them. We could get redress from your father's cruelty. He did it because of his ugly behavior."[7]

This appeal to Titans to seek justice for their father's wrongdoings would be echoed in their offspring. The "call to arms" would signify the transition of power systems according to a "natural behavior law" (since Ouranos was responsible for his downfall). The mythological trope of creating tools for one purpose and having them used by someone else, is also present here.

Chronos would use Adamant to usurp their evil father. This element would eventually become the metal of the gods' choice for their weapons against their evil father, Chronos. The death of Ouranos would allow Gaia to be freed and the Titans to rise, as well as allowing for the creation of more players in this primordial divin theater.

After Gaia gave Chronos an adamant sigle and explained the "stratagem", the moment of separation occurred: "Great Heaven came, bringing about the night, and his son spread himself across the

Earth, stretching out in all directions. His son reached out to the ambush with his left...with his rights he grabbed the massive sickle with its lengthy row of sharp teeth, quickly cutting off his father's male genitals, then flung them behind him so they could fly where they wanted."[8]

Mother Earth and the Titans were both freed from their oppression when the Sky was taken from her. The "drops," as they were called, were what gave birth to the Giants. They were dressed in gleaming armour and held long spears in their hands. Chronos then cut off their genitals. He then threw them in the sea, where they floated on a white foam. The first goddess emerged from this foam (or "Aphros", as ancient Greeks called it). Eros was present during the creation of the first system of power, and Aphrodite, the more complex representation of love, would also be present to welcome in the second.

Sandro Boticelli's painting showing the birth of Aphrodite

Peter Paul Rubens" photo of Chronos, one of his kids, eating

The Titans were liberated from their servitude and in the presence Aphrodite, there was a new surge for reproduction. A new era of gods, rivers and nymphs emerged and took over the roles of their predecessors in the new cosmos. This new cosmos was controlled by the sons & daughters of the evil Ouranos. The offspring of the wicked Ouranos weren't necessarily bad, as they included many deities like Helios (the Sun), Horae ("the Seasons"), and thousands upon thousands of wood- and sea nymphs. This is an important point to remember as we consider the role played by the Titans in their antagonistic role.

Hesiod goes on a long description of the Titans' unions and the fruit they bore. Hesiod then moves to the moment Rhea, "surrendering" to Chronos, gave birth to resplendent children. Hesiod describes the moments when Rhea bore "Hestia. Demeter. and gold-sandaled Hera. Hesiod also mentions the moment that Rhea bore her beautiful children.

Chronos learned from Ouranos's daughter Gaia that it was fated for his defeat by his own child. Hesiod has no explanation as to why his castrated father made this proclamation. He learned from his father that Gaia wasn't trustworthy to imprison her offspring. Therefore, Chronos decided he would devour his children as they were being born. Rhea appealed for help to her parents, Gaia & Ouranos. Gaia suggested that she go to Lyktos in Crete for her birth. Gaia accepted Zeus, the youngest of the gods, and placed him on a mountain. Gaia wrapped the stone in "babycloth", to give to her fervent father. Chronos swallowed and ate the stone, with only a sneaking suspicion that he was about being overthrown, just as his father had done before.

Illustration showing Rhea giving Chronos a stone

Chronos brought each god to life in reverse order. The stone that came first was then taken to Delphi, where it was revered thenceforth. This "rebirthing" of the gods set the scene for a cataclysmic confrontation. They were sentenced to vengeance for their mother's rape and their own imprisonment. Most of the common elements in the cosmos had been created by the original twelve Titans. This provided the foundation for a new order. It was also the place from which all stories-mythological or factual-could be grown and imbued in meaning, according the cosmological order.

The "titanomachy", which was the war against the Titans, was a significant moment in the history of Greek mythological thought. It was the moment the Greeks realized the importance of self-awareness in their own social and intellectual lives.

The term "titanomachy", a compound word, is made up of the Greek words "Machia" and "titan", meaning "fight" and/or "battle". Just like the Amazonomachy and Centauromachy (battles against fearsome Amazons), the Titanomachy is depicted in metopes from the Parthenon, Athens. The metopes included scenes depicting the classic "battles with the other". The Parthenon, a monument, was built following the Persian Wars. This was the largest, most cataclysmic invasion the Greeks had experienced in 700 years. Although the fight was against "the Other", it was a landmark moment in ancient Greek culture and the mind-set of this peculiar group. Their relatively young power systems had beaten an older kingdom with seemingly insurmountable odds. They had overcome these odds and were victorious.

Cornelis Cornelisz-van Haarlem's "The Fall of the Titans."

Joachim Wtewael, "The Battle Between the Gods and the Titans",

Zeus, launching a thunderbolt against the Temple of Artemis at Corfu

Homer and Hesiod were epic poets who "attributed everything that's harmful and blameworthy about men to the divine power: stealing and committing adultery. And deceiving another." [11] However, the Titans were seen as something worse. They embody disorder and hubris.

Although the gods could be prone to human foibles and were innately "human", they were nonetheless progressive. The Titans were "chthonic," representing "Nature" in the battle against the more "cultured"-and certainly, more elaborate-personalities of the Olympian gods, who in this episode, are representative of order and culture.

In the end, the Titanomachy tells the story of rebellion[12] against the old, of culture against nature, of order against chaos. It's a tale that shows a people who has experienced multiple power struggles, and states of unrest. The ancient Greeks, as with many cultures, defined their present state of existence by the "boundary crises" that came before it. [13] This is why the Titanomachy didn't just become a piece of propaganda art, but was a significant moment in ancient Greek cultural history.

The Makings of a Demigod

Many claimed that they had known one of humanity's greatest men during the Age of Heroes. But the poor king of Mycenae is more entitled to this claim than any other. King Electryon is the son of Perseus the great Medusa-slaying Perseus. He was also the grandson Zeus. Yet, eight of his sons were murdered while protecting the king and his cattle from the Teleboans raiding Taphians. In an effort to avenge their deaths he raised an armies and called on King Amphitryon (of Troezen) to come to Mycenae to serve as regent. "When you return, I will have my girl Alcmene as a bride," Electryon shouted to the vanguard and he marched off.

Amphitryon ruled Mycenae in a fair manner, but before long, an unknown caller called his uncle's gates. He claimed to be a representative of the King, Elis, and that he had news that the stolen herd was his. Amphitryon sent his uncle a message to confirm that the herd was his. However, he did not waste any time paying the ransom. Electryon returned to Mycenae angry that his nephew paid ransom for a thief. Amphitryon however was a loyal nephew who refused to listen to his uncle and instead took his frustration out on the cow that had wandered off the herd. The club flew off his hand and hit the cow's horns. This angle was enough to kill King electryon.

Amphitryon and Alcmene had to leave Mycenae, in order to get purification from King Creon. Amphitryon was granted permission by the king. Alcmene, however, refused to share a room with him until he had avenged their deaths. Creon was able to help Amphitryon raise an army that marched against cattle thieves.

Almighty Zeus sat on Mount Olympus and watched the scene with fascination. His attraction to fair Alcmene led him to set his mind to solving his problem. He knew this would not be the last time he would have a son with a mortal. Therefore, he set his mind on creating a hero like none before. Then he sent Hermes out to Helius to ask him to end his celestial wandering. Hermes spoke to the Moon and asked her to slow down so three nights would be one. Then, he assumed the identity of Amphitryon. He flew to Alcmene's bedchamber. He told her - not untruthfully because the true Amphitryon was victorious that day - that his brothers had been avenged and that they had spent the longest nights together. "And she, having fallen in love with both a god a a man exceedingly great, had twin sons in seven gated Thebes. Although they were brothers, they were not one spirit. For one was weaker [Iphicles] and the other was far more powerful, one terrible but strong, the mighty Hercules.

Hercules, the fourth day of the middlewinter month, was born. Hera did not hear the news about Zeus's latest child well, despite Alcmene telling her to name her son Hercules ("Glory and Hera") in order to pacify Hera. Hera, as with all of Zeus's attempts at trying, didn't like the news. So, one night, Zeus sent two azure [15] serpents into Hercules's room. Iphicles alerted their father and shrieked, but Hercules proudly presented them with the dead serpents in a pair of pudgy, untouched hands to the king.

An ancient Roman bust of Hercules strangling and killing a snake

Hercules grew strong and learned from the best teachers. They taught everything from wrestling to augury. He quickly became so adept at augury that he considered vultures to be the best bird, as they never attacked even the smallest living creature. [16] He remained this way throughout his childhood, never attacking, but often found himself in a position to defend the honor of a friend or protect the land from the ravages a beast.

He loved his club more than any other after learning the art of archery from Eurytus. It was made out of the strongest wild olive. He preferred it over his bow whenever possible to demonstrate that his shot was strong.

"Now it became clear that Hercules, following a battle against the Minyans, became jealous of Hera's children and flung them into the fire. Thespius purified him and sent him to Delphi to inquire of the god where to live. The Pythian priestess... instructed him to reside in Tiryns, to serve Eurystheus for twelve year and to perform the ten labors he was required to do.

While the story of Hercules' youth and birth is well-known, modern readers may not be aware of some of the fascinating details. Recent historians have revealed many interesting facts about these episodes. Modern readers find the first shocking point to be Hera's ferocious jealousy of the young man alarming. After all, Hercules was Zeus's last sired child on a mortal wife. His older half brothers never suffered as much as he did at his goddess's hands. This is especially confusing because Hercules's "Glory" name (Glory of Hera) would imply that he would be given her protection. [19] It was not lost on the people who first admired these myths that Hercules's tireless efforts to avoid Hera's wrath were also evident. "Hercules!" in ancient Rome was "Mehercule!" which was an exclamation for surprise and supplication during times of need. In modern English it would be similar to "Good God", or "Mother Of Mercy".

Robert Graves, a poet and historian believed that Hera's animosity with Hercules was rooted within historical events. Some chronological explanations are helpful to better understand it. Graves stated that Alcmene could have been a Mycenaean title, for Hera, and meant "Strong in Wrath."[20] The Mycenaean Period (1600-1100 BCE), a period of Greek History, is marked by the unification among people around palace centers like Mycenae (Tiryns), Thebes, Athens, and Tiryns. It was during this period, that mainland Greeks developed strong cultural identities apart from the Minoans, who previously ruled over Crete. Graves suggested the Hercules myth names are like shadows from former religious groups of the Mycenaean Era. Alcmene/Hera is associated with Mycenae. Graves also allocates the "Glory of Hera" to the cult as a guardian figure. Perseus is the name of an Achaean cult which means "Destroyer" and eventually overcame Mycenaean. Perseus adopted Hercules into House of Perseus. Graves described Hera's "humbled" state as the moment when the mythographers first began to use the animosity she felt towards Hercules. This happened at the end the Mycenaean Period, in the 10thcentury BCE. The appearance of the people known as "the Dorians" in archaeological records coincides with major cultural (mainly in terms of burial practices and iron workings) changes. The Dorians worshipped Hercules. They developed strong connections with his offspring the Heracleids and were, perhaps because of their iron working connection, considered very warlike and austere.

Hercules's twin birth is a very common theme in the myths and legends of the ancient heroes. It highlights Hercules's mythic "universality". [21] Hercules's story can be connected to the stories of other Mediterranean cultures. From the imitation of Alcmene's husband, Zeus, in order to get sex with her--which is a predominantly Egyptian theme[22]-–to the connections made with the heroes and heroines of the Near East. Graves specifically noted that "It may have been assumed that the central tale of Hercules is an early variant the Babylonian Gilgamesh epi - which reached Greece through Phoenicia."[23].

The Phoenicians were particularly passionate worshippers of Melqart. Later, the Greeks came to associate Melqart's god with their own. Herodotus wrote in his Histories that "Moreover, in order to get clear information regarding this matter where it was possible, I boarded a ship for Tyre, Phoenicia. Here I inquired about the existence of a holy temple dedicated to Hercules. It was richly adorned with many other offerings. The temple also had two pillars: one of refined and one of gold. At night, it shone brightly. In conversation with the priests I inquired how long it had been since it was built. It was also not consistent with the Greeks' belief. They said that the temple dedicated to the god was built in Tyre when it was founded. That was two thousand and three hundred centuries ago. I found another temple of Thasian Hercules in Tyre. I also went to Thasos where I discovered another temple of Hercules. These were Phoenicians who built it during their expeditions to Europe. I believe they had done so five generations prior the birth of Hercules (son of Amphitryon) in Hellas. What I found by asking questions clearly proves that

Hercules, the son of Amphitryon in Hellas, is an ancient god.

This means Hercules's story was known and fleshed up as early as the 5thcentury BCE, when Herodotus began writing. Also, by that time, his connection with the number four was also established. According to myth, Hercules was first connected to the Olympic Games. He was said to have created them. Walter Burkert, the historian, pointed out that Hercules' festivals, unlike those in Olympia were not held to one city-state or even polis. They were instead organized by cults independent of the political entity. [25] Each four years, the Olympic Games witnessed a cessation or hostilities among political entities. This was another example Hercules 'universality.

A common folkloric cliché is that Hercules is shown as indefatigable. [26] However elements of a character's dad can often be seen ostensibly in their son's subtext. To the ancient reader, Hercules, the son of Zeus would have exuded royalty, and inspired the human desire in wish-fulfillment stories. Therefore, his enslavement may seem even more paradoxical that his name.

The Labours

Roman relief from antiquity depicting the Labours or Hercules.

"First, Eurystheus directed him to bring along the skin of Nemean lion; the Nemean was an invulnerable animal begotten from Typhon. To attack the lion, his route took him to Cleonae where he lodged at Molorchus' house as a day laborer. Hercules instructed him to wait for thirty more days and then to sacrifice to Saviour Zeus if his hunt was over. If he died, he would sacrifice himself to Zeus as a hero. After tracking down the lion,

Hercules shot the first arrow but realized the beast was invulnerable. Hercules came to Nemea and found the lion hiding in a cave with both mouths. He built the second entrance and came in on the beast through the first. Holding his arm around its neck, he choked it, so he threw it onto his shoulders and carried it to Cleonae.

An ancient illustration of Hercules fighting against the Nemean lion

Peter Paul Rubens' painting shows Hercules fighting against the Nemean Lion.

Molorchus was only about to make Hercules' first sacrifice when he arrived in Cleonae. He stopped, took heart in the sight of the great man holding the beast, and hugged him eagerly. They both offered their sacrifices to Zeus and Hercules used one the lion's claws as a cutting tool to remove the skin. He carried the shield around his body and traveled to

Tiryns for Eurystheus. Eurystheus was astonished to see Hercules approach the gate. The king was terrified and immediately closed the city's gates. Hercules was barred from entering the city again. In the meantime, he ordered his courtsmiths to make a bronze Urn and place it in a ground for the king. Hercules would receive his instructions at a safe distance from the city.

Hercules first labour was not remarkable by mythological standards. The classicist G.S. includes the hunt, capture, possible killing, and possibly slaying, of a beast possessing supernatural powers. In this case, it is an impenetrable skin. Kirk's "commonest topics" in mythology. This theme is "Fulfillment Of A Task or Quest", which Kirk says is the essence of Hercules's tale. Kirk was aware of the lack of "imagination" in Greek mythology and saw Hercules as an example. Hercules is ancient Greece's greatest hero. He noted that Greek myths were "drawn up from many sources and for many reasons." Sometimes, one can see a special motive behind a particular theme, such an aetiological motive. Or sometimes the reflection of a serious preoccupation. These schematic qualities are evident... but it is important to remember that the rest of heroic mythology isn't essentially different."[28]

Kirk recognizes Hercules 12 labours. He refers to it as a "Babylonian mindset" because the number was so important in their calendars and mathematical systems. Kirk's work is very similar to J.G. Robert Graves and Frazer. These two scholars were advocates for the "Sacred King," which had a profound impact on their work on world mythology. According to those who supported the theory, the "Sacred Kingdom" was a ritualistic position that the king assumed upon taking office. His rule was divinely granted, but his approach to office, actions in office and termination of his "rule", all were strictly controlled according to socio-religious customs. You could have expected the king to atone by working hard, or perhaps he was responsible for certain agricultural signs, such as "attaining the office" during the growing season and "ending" during harvest. Some proponents of this theory believed that, given the great antiquity of the "Sacred King" as a sociological position, this "end" could have originally been actual human sacrifice, which was later mythologized and came to be a symbolic/mythological act instead.

Graves regards this labour as Hercules's initial act as a "Sacred Queen". He mentions that ritual combat against beasts was a common occurrence for "Sacred Kings" in Greece and Asia Minor,

Babylonia, Syria, and Babylonia. According to the culture, the animals were diverse, but each was representative for one of the four seasons. Hercules's labours include the vanquishing of four beasts-- representative of a four-season year--of which the lion was the first. The "Sacred King", by defeating these beasts, was able to "conquer the" year(s). [29]

Pindar, a poet who wrote in the 5th century BCE, claimed that sacrifices were made during his time to Hercules both as a hero (and then later as a god) - a fact Herodotus confirmed in his analysis.

Hercules's duality went beyond his status as demigod. He was also destined to be a god at his death, which is a frequent theme in his story. His "conquering" death is an aspect of his "godliness", which will be featured in many of his stories. The "two mouthed cave" symbolises the intermediary space between mortality and immortality, between the eternal and the inexorable. Hercules begins his journey to "ritual" death, and his apotheosis when he conquers both entrances of the lion.

"Men say Typhon, the horrifying, outrageous and lawless, was smitten in love with her, a maid with glancing eye [Echidna], Mother Of Monsters]. So she was able to bear and bring forth fierce offspring...the evil-minded Hydra Of Lerna, whom the goddess, white arm Hera, nourished, being furious with the mighty Hercules.

www.ingramcontent.com/pod-product-compliance
Lightning Source LLC
Chambersburg PA
CBHW050404120526
44590CB00015B/1814